MW00682458

Beauty
Resp nse
to Cancer

In keeping with Neveen Dominic's philanthropic spirit, proceeds from the sale of this book will be donated to Beauty Response to Cancer Society and projects benefiting South Sudanese refugees around the world.

Thank you for your generous support.

"The story told in this book is at once harrowing and hopeful, heartbreaking and full of joy. Beginning a world away, with vividly detailed refugee experiences most of us would find unimaginable, the book takes us along on Neveen Dominic's journey to success in Canada, with a riveting narrative punctuated by such unexpected delights as beauty tips and delectable Sudanese recipes."

Irene Moore Davis
MA English Literature

"We love everything about South Sudanese philanthropist Neveen Dominic's Collection. The Juba® Dual Powder Pallet is perfect to set, add coverage or for touch ups. The gentle, silky substance will glide over your skin without settling into fine lines. Offering a range of dark foundations, this was designed with African-American skin tones in mind and aims to expand makeup kits for all clients "

MAKE-UP ARTIST Magazine
October/November 2017 issue

The following are review transcripts that were given by video at the Juba Collection® Launch in New York, New York on April 7, 2017.

"It is important for makeup artists to have makeup products like the Juba foundations. I tested on my skin and it has that right balance of sheen and being matte. It looks like skin and not makeup that is sitting on top of skin. The first time I ever applied makeup on a black person was on the great Gregory Hines when I was at NBC Studios. When I saw him, I was saying oh my God and oh my goodness. I thought wow, ok. I really didn't know what to do for him. He said just do something under the eyes and that is about all I need. I said ok but had no idea what he wanted under the eyes. I took one of three colours in my kit and chose the darkest one and put it under his eyes. Being the gracious man that he is, Gregory took a look in the mirror, shook my hands and said you are a magician. He walked out and probably went to the men's room to remove whatever I put on his face. I decided right then and there that I needed to understand how to do black skin and I need the right products to do so. I wish there was a pallet like the Juba pallet at that time because it would have probably been what he would have gravitated to right away."

Michael Key
CEO of Key Publishing Group
Emmy Award Winning Makeup Artist
Publisher of Makeup Artist Magazine
Producer of International Makeup Artist Trade Show - IMATS

Beauty from the Ashes of War

"These products represent the darker skin that has been totally dismissed. In the fashion industry, dark skin models are experiencing a problem getting their makeup done properly. This company is more than cosmetics, it empowers and lives to inspire."

Mari Malek
New York Super Model and Activist

To: Silivia

Thank you for your
support

NEVEEN
DOMINIC

BEAUTY FROM THE
ASHES OF WAR

A Testimony of God's Love and Dreams Come True

Neveen Dominic – Beauty from the Ashes of War
Copyright © 2018 by Neveen Dominic

Published by Neveen Dominic
www.neveendominic.com
Cover Design and Layout by: Enyinnaya Emmanuel Jr
Koolzzy278 Graphics

Editor: Ruth Yesmaniski
Co Editor: Charles Ohwode

Cover Photo: Kenneth Fung
Portfolio Photo: Rafal Wegiel

Printed in Canada
ISBN – 978-1-7752368-0-1

DEDICATION

This book is dedicated to God for saving my life.

To my parents who have inspired me to be a humanitarian and entrepreneur and to strive for excellence in my career despite the challenges and difficulties that I face.

To my immediate family who are my inspiration and motivation.

To my South Sudanese community for becoming my extended family.

ACKNOWLEDGEMENTS

I am as good as my team. My deepest gratitude to God for giving me an opportunity to have an enabling platform where I can share my story and be an inspiration to others. I am humbled to be surrounded by a group of amazing people who come to my aid every time that I need them. I am extremely thankful to my family, friends and mentors who took time out of their very busy schedules to help with research on Beauty From The Ashes of War.

Special thanks to my mother Teresina Batikayo, my editors Ruth Yesmaniski and Charles Ohwode and my graphic artist Emmanuel Enyinnaya Jr. for their dedication, commitment, advice and support during the writing of this book. Many thanks also to Gabriel Dominic, Irene Moore Davis and Amira Makeer.

I also want to give a special thanks to all of my fans and supporters for inspiring me to have the courage to put my story into writing.

I could not have done it without you.

About the Author

Hailing from South Sudan, Neveen Dominic often struggled to find cosmetic products made for her ebony skin tone. With so many cosmetic companies touting their foundations' "wide range" of skin tones, Dominic was often let down when she found that these same companies' color ranges so often stopped short at "mocha." She remembers the days she struggled to find any products to suit her skin tone and although she was passionate about beauty, the limited product choices made it hard to achieve that "glam" look every girl dreams of. The job of perfecting the complexion is even more daunting for dark skinned women, who often have to perfect intricate makeup techniques or are left without being able to wear makeup at all. She noticed that even professional makeup artists shied away from taking clients with deep skin tones because of the limitations in their own product offerings. When Neveen saw other dark skinned women turn towards extreme methods such as skin bleaching to fit more Eurocentric standards of beauty, she knew that the issue was more than skin deep.

Fed up with having to compromise, Mrs. Dominic created Neveen Dominic Cosmetics™ with the goal of making all women look and feel beautiful, regardless of skin tone. The philanthropist and entrepreneur had a vision for celebrating and embracing multifaceted beauty and making accessible cosmetics for diverse women.

Table of Contents

Endorsement   i

Title Page   iv

Copyright Page   v

Dedication   vi

Acknowledgements   vii

About the author   vii

Introduction   1

Chapter 1   South Sudan   7

Chapter 2   Moving to the North   23

Chapter 3   Our Home in Sudan   37

Chapter 4   Refugee in Egypt   45

Chapter 5   Basketball   67

Chapter 6   The United Nations Aid   79

Chapter 7   Coming to North America   89

Chapter 8   The Wave   121

Chapter 9   Neveen Dominic Cosmetics™   131

Chapter 10   The Juba Collection   151

Letter to the Egyptian People   154

Recipes   158

Portfolio   162

Coupons   174

Appendix/ References   178

INTRODUCTION

As we come from different backgrounds and walks of life, sometimes we feel that no one understands what we are going through or what we are trying to do. This is absolutely true.

As no one truly understands your struggles, I hope you know that some can imagine it. Even though this book is not for everyone, my desire is to share with people who can relate to my pain or can imagine what I went through. In telling my story, I hope that it inspires you to see a way out of your situation if you are in a difficult place, to strive for new heights in your career or business, or to be proud of who you are and what you are capable of doing.

This book is written for to the following people:

For the woman who had to sacrifice so much, including her happiness in the name of marriage, tradition, ambition or pleasing family members. She experiences little joy, but is doing her best to make her way through this thing called 'life' in order to be viewed as a good wife, mother, or someone who came from a good family.

For the war victim or survivor who could not see light at the end of the tunnel or hope for a normal life or a bright future. The person who has been bullied, abused or their life has been threaten or they have gone through a near death experience. Life looks different in his/her eyes compared to others who live in a bubble in the so called "safe parts of the world."

For South Sudanese people all over the world, especially the youth battling the war, ones who are still in refugee camps or those just trying to find a better life. There is a brighter day coming to us as a South Sudanese nation regardless of where we are currently residing. Our past cannot define us but what we do in the present is what will ensure a good future for us and the generations to come. It is time to put our differences aside and for us to see each other as one. I am looking forward to working with like-minded South Sudanese people to help rebuild our land and people. We can no longer say "someone needs to do something about what is going on in South Sudan!" That someone is you and I. We understand our problems better than anyone else and it is time for us to work together and solve them.

For people who desire peace and to make the world a better place. Your philanthropic and humanitarian personalities are what will plant seeds into people and build them up. To bring positive change to the world, we need to start by upgrading our mindset. Be a blessing to others in whatever capacity you can. We all have power. It is up to us to use it however we can to impact one another. The work you are doing is beyond just lending a hand to someone. You are saving lives even by just smiling at someone or giving them a compliment to make them feel good for the moment. No one may have ever told them something that nice. They may have been on a suicide mission and your compliment was everything they needed to hear to see value in life. Keep planting the good seed as someone will always water it. With the multiplier effect, we can all make the world a better place by focusing on impacting one person.

For the entrepreneur who knows that he/she has what it takes to be successful in business. Regardless of whether people believe in you or not, you are willing to take the risk and do whatever it takes to be successful. You have been called 'crazy', your ideas are 'stupid' or 'it will never work'. You know that the best way to rise above the people who never believed in you, or try to put you down, is to be way more successful than they have ever imagined or given you credit for. You are a visionary and you see what others are not capable of seeing and that is why you understand why they do not understand you or your ideas. When people see how successful your ideas are, they will stop calling you crazy and start calling you brilliant. You would rather be respected than loved, anyways, if you cannot have both. It is also for the entrepreneur who wants to start a business and doesn't know how.

For the person that follows their passion no matter what others think about it. You know that a fulfilling career is one that is built on passion and not status or pay cheque size. Going to work every day inspires you and you look forward to every project with excitement. You take a lot of pride in your work and take time to appreciate the art in successfully completing it and having others appreciate it. You are so happy with what you are doing that you are known for even doing it for free at times.

For people who grow and learn from their experiences, especially negative ones. You do not let your past enslave you but celebrate that it is over, while looking forward to the beginning of healing for a better future. Your past does not define you, but your personality and attitude do.

For the person who does not believe in God and the believer who can see God's love in my testimony. If God can do it for me, He can do it for you too.

It is for my cancer clients struggling with the cosmetic side effects of treatments, and for others with debilitating diseases or health issues that make them feel like they are less beautiful than they really are.

For those who want to know the personality behind the Neveen Dominic Cosmetics™ brand. Healthy relationships are built on transparency and trust. This is my opportunity to tell you about the real me and things I care about. If you don't know where I came from, it will be difficult for you to see where I am going.

Chapter 1

South Sudan

South Sudan is one of the most beautiful countries in the world. It is located in East-Central Africa, surrounded by Sudan, Ethiopia, Uganda, Kenya, the Republic of Congo, and the Central African Republic. Ninety percent of South Sudan lays along the River Nile and features many beautiful landmarks including national parks, the infamous Sudd Swamp, and the world's largest animal migration in Boma National Park. Despite its natural beauty, civil wars have been going on in South

Beauty from the Ashes of War

Sudan for decades. It became the Republic of South Sudan when it gained independence in 2011. Despite gaining its independence with 98.83% of the votes, the country is still in a civil war since 2013, suffering ethnic violence. Over sixty indigenous languages are spoken in South Sudan. Each tribe has its own culture and religious beliefs.

Neveen Dominic was born in Juba, now the capital of South Sudan. She is the eldest of seven children and the proud mother of three. Her father was a humanitarian and politician who believed in equality and freedom. He was the first to graduate from school in his village. He went on to receive a PHD in political science in Rome which exposed him to opportunities to travel to many European and African countries. He valued education and ensured that he provided the best he possibly could for his family. Her mother is a high school graduate who has been involved in various business ventures over the course of many years. Neveen grew up wanting to make her parents and family proud. She cherished the values her parents instilled in her and continues to use them as her guide to live by, as she passes them down to her children.

Growing up in South Sudan was difficult to say the least, living in a constant state of panic and anxiety which affected everyone including Neveen and her family. The atmosphere was charged with fear and everyone's life was threatened because of the civil war. Beauty and fashion were insignificant in the

South Sudanese society at that time. The most important things were survival and education.

Children went to school wearing uniforms. There were only two hairstyles that were permitted for students from kindergarten to elementary, through to intermediate and senior schools. Boys wore their hair in a buzz cut and girls either wore their hair in cornrows straight back or in a buzz cut like the boys. Not only was this due to the extreme heat in South Sudan but it was also meant to keep students focused on their studies and not on fashion, beauty or the opposite sex. Nails were kept groomed with no nail polish for girls, just manicured and kept clean. Uniforms were required to be clean and ironed. Teachers would check students in the morning, every day, to ensure that the students were clean and well-groomed according to the school's expectations. The boys and girls were inspected for head lice as well. Personal hygiene and grooming were extremely important in school. Students who did not comply with school rules and regulations regarding personal hygiene and grooming were sent home to prepare properly before coming back to school.

Succeeding in school was every student's concern in South Sudan. Most students studied hard and appreciated the education their parents could afford to provide for them. Education was a privilege; not many parents could afford to send their children to school. Of the children who could not go to school, some went to the village to help their parents with farming and other labor intensive trades. Children who could go to school were viewed as higher class members of society.

The end of the year was a very exciting but also scary moment for students and their families. The top ten honor students in the school and in their class were celebrated grandly at school, by their relatives at home and by the neighborhood where they lived. Parents would have very big parties and celebrate their children's success. However, the opposite was true for students who came last and second to last in their class.

That day was one of the worst days of their lives. A parade of shame was kicked off at their school. Classmates would follow them in a crowd and would let everyone know that they came last or second to last. Results were normally announced in a count-down, openly, for the top 10 starting from the tenth to the first. The rest of the report cards were handed out according to the averages from highest to lowest; even though the averages were not called out. The last student to receive their report card was called "Al Teesh" and the student before him or her was "Naip Al Teesh,"(who was only disgraced at school and not followed home). As the parade of shame approached the Al Teesh's home, the neighborhood kids would join the parade and the student would become the laughing stock of the community, usually receiving beatings from their family members and neighbors for bringing shame to the family and neighborhood. The idea was to get the student to work harder and improve his or her studies and strive for better grades.

Al Teesh did not always have a failed grade. In the event that Al Teesh did not fail the exams with a mark that was below the passing grade of 50%, no parade was allowed to follow him or her home. This was the academic culture with the attitude of failure not being an option to the student, the school, the family and the community. This culture is no longer practiced in South Sudan today.

Young girls in South Sudan were trained at home by their parents to excel in domestic house work. They helped their mothers with chores around the house and helped take care of their fathers and siblings. The average family size was ten, including the parents. Some South Sudanese tribes practiced polygamy as part of their culture. Their average family size was thirty.

Girls who were very good at domestic house work were known in the community and they got married first. Their husbands paid higher dowries for them. Daughters were their family's assets and pride. A young girl growing up did not only help her family with domestic chores at home, she also sold products in the open market or provided paid services to help with the financial needs of the family. Her skills and education were carefully considered when her family asked for her dowry before marriage. The more educated the girl was, the higher her bride price was. The family viewed a marriage suitor as someone who was going to take away their helper and provider. That meant there would be no one to fill the void that the daughter had filled. The dowry was a compensation to the family for their loss. Sometimes the dowry was money, land, a farm, cows or a combination of all assets. To remove the daughter who was an asset to the family, a different asset was required to be given in its place to compensate the family.

Girls were trained to conduct themselves in a manner that brought honor and dignity to their family. The requisite was that the bride must be a virgin at the time of their marriage and a proof of virginity was often required. Premarital relationships were not common in the South Sudanese society. Marriage suitors would propose first to the girl's father prior to talking to the girl. Being attracted to the husband or his age were irrelevant to families. The most important consideration was the husband-to-be's ability to provide for his wife-to-be and to give her the same comfort she had had in her father's house or to be provided with an even better quality of life.

Marriage in South Sudan was considered to be the highest honor for every girl and a dream-come-true. The husband was also expected to make sure that his in-laws were doing well and that he would take care of them for as long as he was married to the daughter. A girl who was not a virgin was returned to her family and the husband could return her to her father's house the following day after the marriage and demand for the return of his dowry as she was considered "damaged." This was the most shameful event in the life of South Sudanese women. Some women would commit suicide in those events. Some became prostitutes because everyone in the community would know that they were damaged. Their family would be buried in shame and they would throw her out of the house.

Besides being a virgin, a South Sudanese woman was expected to be able to produce many children for her husband. It was his return on his dowry investment. The more children the better. A big family was considered to be a wealthy family especially if they had many girls. Girls often got married after or during high school. It was considered to be the prime time for men's enjoyment. Girls were considered to be a property of their parents and when they got married they became a property of their husbands. This culture is also no longer practiced in South Sudan today. With the war spreading South Sudanese people as refugees all over the world, family cultures and traditions are overriding tribal cultural views on marriage.

The best compliment any woman could get in South Sudan was to be asked if she was a new bride.

Brides were viewed as the most beautiful and radiant women in the South Sudanese society. The six month beauty process that Sudanese and South Sudanese women went through was the best experience of their lives. Young girls were transitioned during this period to be the best version of themselves and were taught to transition from a young girl to a responsible woman. They would have daily spa services and pampering by their mother's, relatives and friends. Services included sugaring, exfoliation, hair treatments, pedicures and manicures, massage and "dukhan" which was a unique sauna experience with two types of woods known as "Taleeh and Shaf". These woods had unique health benefits to bones, body and skin. Brides had a unique type of glow from the inside out. Their hair was soft, stylish and shiny. Their skin was smooth, bright and flawless. There was a special type of incense known as "Kabarate" that was prepared with family secret recipes which was burnt at the bride-to-be's house, during all bridal events and at her new house. There was a special soft exfoliant that was also prepared to be used on the bride's skin known as "Delka." A special type of perfume was also made for the bride, bridal party, and married women in the community to wear to the bride's three days of marriage known as "Khumra."

Henna was a huge part of the wedding celebration and events. It was one of the events where all women including the young girls could get their henna art done for the wedding. The henna design was elaborate and was drawn on both hands of the bride and her feet as well. Some of the henna ingredients like "Mahlabeia" was imported from India for the occasion. The South Sudanese henna is black in comparison to the Indian henna which is orange. During the henna event, a singer was hired to sing live with a band. The bride's husband-to-be also would get a henna done in most cultures but only on his hands and not in a design or pattern. The bride was then dressed in gold accessories purchased by her husband which would amount to hundreds of thousands of Sudanese pounds. Her makeup was done glamorously and she would be dancing to the live singing for her husband who was the only male in attendance of the "women only" event. It was an entertaining dance by the bride for her husband-to-be and the guests. This dance was very important and the bride was well trained for it. It was a passionate dance and an expression of love.

Day two of the marriage celebration was the traditional marriage and it was celebrated differently according to the tribal tradition of the bride. The bride wore her traditional outfit and so did her family. Her husband and his family also did the same. The two families joined and celebrated as one family along with their neighbors.

Day three was the white wedding where the bride wore a white gown and was married in church or according to their religious beliefs. On that day a lot of food and drinks were prepared as it was seen as a time to dine and celebrate as one new family and community. That was also the day that the bride would lose her virginity to her husband as it would be her first time experiencing intimacy with a man. The day after the marriage was called "Soupeya". It was a day that the families and close friends gathered to find out if all went well with the evening as a newlywed couple. It is a day that can be the most glorious day in the couples' lives or the most disgraceful day for the bride. If all went well, the celebration would continue and the husband's family would shower the bride with gifts and money. They would also be looking for the news of pregnancy soon after the wedding. If she was not found a virgin, the celebrations were stopped and the refund process of her dowry would start immediately. The husband and his family would be disappointed and would call the girl damaged.

Neveen's parents' marriage was an arranged marriage. Her grandfather was an accountant at a bank and he viewed her father, who was a client, as a perfect marriage suitor for his daughter. Neveen's mother was in her late teens, her father was ten years older than she was. He was educated and was financially well-established. He also had moved home from overseas and was more civilized than the average South Sudanese man. Her grandfather thought that he would provide a comfortable home and good quality of life for his daughter. Her mother was not attracted to her husband-to-be but she chose to be obedient, and married him to make her father happy. Even though she never enjoyed her marriage she couldn't leave her children or disappoint her father. If she chose to leave Neveen's father, according to tradition, she would have to leave the children behind. She did not want her children to suffer. They were from two different tribes in Equatoria state in South Sudan. She sacrificed her entire life on the altar of her marriage and dedicated it to providing the best for her children.

Due to the lifestyle and expectations of girls, beauty and fashion were only considered once in a while for special occasions but was mostly an area of interest for prostitutes who needed the it to solicit themselves and their services. Fashionable items were normally purchased by the girl's parents to make sure that they were decent and appropriate. If someone saw a girl in the market or on the street dressed too fashionably or inappropriately, they would ask her if her parents had seen her when she left the house. Some would discipline the girl in public and let it be as a warning and some would also come home and ask to meet with the father to discuss his daughter's dressing as they saw it. Self-respect and decency were huge values in the South Sudanese society. Traditional clothing was designed by each tribe to represent the tribe and to give a guide to its people when they were in public. Aside from every tribe having its own tribal clothing, they also had their own language, body markings, food and culture.

When visitors came to Juba, they saw different tribes wearing their various traditional clothing and all looked different. They were able to identify which tribe a South Sudanese person was from because of the way they were dressed, what they were eating, the tribal marks on their faces or bodies, and what topics of conversation they were engaged in. People were very content with their traditions and values. They did not mix much with other South Sudanese tribes, whether through friendship or marriage, in order to preserve their own tribal culture. There were tribes who would marry specific tribes only and some who would not approve of marriage or relationship solely because of the tribe that the other person was from. A lot of issues in South Sudan started due to intermixing with other tribes. Often, the traditions were not the same. It was like marrying someone from another country.

The South Sudanese community was very involved in family affairs. They helped children to attend school and assisted them with their studies. They approved relationships and marriages and shared celebrations with families.

When families had conflicts and issues which could not be resolved at home, the elders of the community would mediate to resolve the problems and maintain order in the community. With the inter-tribal marriages, the family dynamic continued to change and things were getting out of control. Conflicts went from

Beauty from the Ashes of War

families against each other to communities against each other. With the multiplier effect it became what it is today. A lot of these conflicts stemmed from lack of education, ignorance and inherited hatred.

The government was also a huge part of the national tribal conflict. Before South Sudan became an independent country, the government of northern Sudan oppressed the South Sudanese people. They deprived them of education and extracted the natural resources of South Sudan. South Sudanese people had the lowest paid jobs which were labor intensive and they were treated like second class citizens in their own country. They were often bullied and mistreated at work. Violence and excessive force were used when dealing with South Sudanese people. Villages were attacked by the Sudanese army and atrocities were committed against the innocent villagers and their families. The situation was beyond the resolution of the elders of the communities and the governors of the states in South Sudan. These injustices caused the South Sudanese people to form their own army against the Sudanese government.

South Sudanese Liberation Army – SPLA was an army that was led by Dr. John Garang in the second Sudanese Civil War. The war took place until South Sudan became an independent country. Instead of bringing peace, however, the war re-ignited soon after South Sudan's independence. The war caused South Sudanese people to seek refuge in neighboring cities and countries. Safety and survival were every South Sudanese family's priority. Not everyone could afford escaping due to financial reasons or for fear of the unknown because they had never traveled outside their village or city. Some were also afraid of running into the government army or rebels and having atrocities committed against them and their families or getting caught in the crossfire between the two groups. Terror was everywhere. Some people decided to face the war instead of leaving so they stayed in their homes. The result was genocide and complete chaos in the villages. Juba became over populated. People who could not afford to travel walked to neighboring countries like Ethiopia and Kenya.

Cases of kidnapping children was increasingly high in South Sudan during the war. Militants used this crime to initiate children into the army. Around that period, the government declared war against South Sudanese boys. They wanted to kill all the boys so that they did not face them as men. Many atrocities were committed against male children forcing boys to run away to be safe. Many children between the ages of seven and ten walked thousands of miles without parents, food, water or medication of any kind to seek refuge in countries such as Ethiopia and Kenya. Their families were killed in their villages and they were left to survive on their own. They were called the lost boys. Because of the war that was declared on them, they had to become child soldiers and fight in the war. They had to face hunger, thirst, wild animals, government soldiers, rebel soldiers and the Ethiopian and Kenyan soldiers. Even at the borders they faced militants and were either killed or were forced into the army to be traitors who then provided information about the locations of civilians and rebels. This started in the 1980's.

As a politician, Neveen's father had just gained some political power after his election when he moved home from overseas. He and his family's lives were placed in danger because of the new position. It meant that he too had to relinquish his political office, leave the war region and move to North Sudan to live peacefully with his family. At the same time, he also hoped to provide a better quality of life for his immediate family in the new region.

Chapter 2

Moving to the North

On moving to northern Sudan with her family due to the civil war in South Sudan and the dangers that it posed to her father because of his political affiliations, Neveen and her family found their new home in the capital city of Khartoum.

Khartoum was a predominantly Muslim city, unlike Juba. Most women covered their hair wearing hijab and long dresses or skirts with long sleeves all year-round including during summer. Some also covered their faces. Life in the north was very different than what they had become accustomed to in South Sudan. The first thing Neveen noticed was the much greater emphasis on women's beauty, fashion and style. The north Sudanese women in Khartoum were lighter in complexion and they were very fashionable even though they were not prostitutes. Neveen was very fascinated by this discovery. She admired the colors, textures, designs, styles and makeup of the women. Not only was their complexion different but so was their hair. It was long and kinky. Some women also had straight and curly hair which was very different than South Sudanese hair which is nappy. Her parents reminded her of who she was and the kind of family she came from. She understood that every time she walked out of the house, she was representing her parents and family. As fascinating as fashion and beauty were, Neveen understood that she was in Khartoum temporarily until the war was over. She needed to maintain her cultural values and focus on succeeding in school and bringing honor to herself and her family.

Neveen always strove for perfection, and continues to do so, even to the present. She did everything with passion and commitment. She took a lot of pride in her work, always desiring to make her parents and the elders of her community proud. She was consistently one of the top 10 honour students in her school and sometimes even in the city. Neveen enjoyed her father's bragging about her to his friends and their excitement to meet her. At times, the pressure was intense because there was direct competition, but her father pushed her to work harder and do better.

The first house where Neveen and her family lived was in a suburban neighborhood in Khartoum. Their neighbors were Muslims and were close to each other. Neveen experienced not only the culture shock but bullying as well by the neighborhood kids because she didn't wear hijab like the rest of them and she was a Christian. What was worse was that she wore pants, shorts and T-shirts which were considered to be inappropriate in the north Sudanese culture. Neveen was spared the full force of the bullying because she didn't see the neighbors' children often as she went to a private Catholic charter school, St. Francis Elementary School, while the Muslim children went to a public school. St. Francis Elementary School had multicultural students, mainly foreigners, from all over the world. Her father wanted to provide the best possible education for his kids. Their family had a driver that took Neveen and her siblings to school as well as a full house staff including a cook, maids and tutors to assist Neveen and her siblings to excel academically. They were often challenged with homework and projects above and beyond the school's expectations. There was never a day that there was no homework at school or at home.

Neveen's father was working for Sudan Aid at the time. He was providing humanitarian assistance to

South Sudanese war survivors settling in Khartoum. As the need for humanitarian assistance continued to rise and many of her extended family needed help, Neveen's father had to make substantial cuts to all the privileges the family had been enjoying. He put his children in public school and cut all the house staff. He also sold his cars and started taking public transportation. Neveen and her siblings walked to school from that time on.

Neveen's mother was a brave and very strong woman. She was not as educated as her husband but she had the business and hustling mentality. She was an amazing mother and partner. She supported all of her husband's endeavors and sacrificed everything for her children because her husband was very focused on his relatives' and community's needs.

As the war got worse, more people started moving to Khartoum. A lot of them could barely afford the bus fare to move to the north. They borrowed the money most of the time, with the hope of getting a job in Khartoum and paying the money back. Moving to Northern Sudan opened new opportunities for Neveen's family. Her father was working for Sudan Aid as he spoke twenty-three languages including tribal languages. He was an asset to the organization and to his community. People heard about his contributions in helping South Sudanese people settle in the north. Many of his voters, friends, church members, family, neighbors, admirers, and even strangers would find a way to contact him and ask for help. He was happy to help as many people as he could and was proud of the impact he was making in his community. When he exhausted all the resources from work, he opened his home to assist many people who were in difficult situations.

Eventually, Neveen's family had to move to an average neighborhood to stretch out their resources and help more people. By this time there were forty people from different tribes from all over Sudan living in Neveen's house. The home became a refugee camp for South Sudanese war survivors and they all lived as one big happy family.

Neveen's father was influential and had very good ties with the Catholic Church. The church often supported his humanitarian efforts and they trusted him. He had studied theology in Rome when he earlier had wanted to become a Catholic priest and he loved helping his people. The new neighborhood that Neveen lived in was warm and the neighbors loved and supported each other. The elders of the community helped Neveen's mother secure a piece of land as it was a new neighborhood. The land was given almost free and the house was built. It was a big house and it was perfect for everyone. The neighbors were very hospitable and they treated each other like extended family. People borrowed things like salt, soap, spices and whatever they needed from each other instead of running to the store or to the market to buy things they needed. It was a high context and collective culture which was a culture that focused on relationships and the welfare of the community instead of individualistic agendas. Everyone in the neighborhood knew each other including relatives that visited the neighborhood. When a stranger visited the neighborhood, everyone would know and be on alert. When someone was visiting a neighbor for the first time, they would introduce him or her to the neighbors, usually by having a get together at their home. It would be huge news and everyone would be excited to meet the visitor and would come bringing gifts. The environment was safe and welcoming.

The neighborhood routine was as follows:
People woke up at 4 am for prayers as they were Muslims. Everyone would clean up their houses and be ready to walk to school, take the bus to work or go to the market. School started at 6 am and was done at noon. The sun was very hot so it was best to be home before it got too hot between noon and 3 pm. Being in the sun during these hours made people susceptible to heat stroke "Sahawi"; which required fluid extraction from patients' spines. Sudanese people had only tea when they woke up in the morning. Some may have also taken it with a fried dumpling or a small piece of bread. Breakfast was at 10 am and it was usually made of beans, a meal also known as "Fool" in the Middle East. Sudanese people are well known for making the best Fool which they call "Muzabat". The beans were seasoned with spices to which fresh salad ingredients

were added except for lettuce as it did not grow in Sudan. Ingredients like yogurt were also added sometimes, but not always. Almost everyone in Sudan had fool every single day for breakfast and sometimes for dinner, either at their houses or at a restaurant. It was the national Sudanese breakfast. Other food that was consumed sometimes was "Tamia" known as falafel in the Middle East.

Neveen would have a fool sandwich every day for breakfast at school, which was packed from home. She would eat in a group with friends. They used to make something called "Fata" which was a mix of all the sandwiches brought to school by her and her friends. They would cut up their sandwiches in small bites and mix them so that each person could taste everyone else's food.

When school was dismissed, every student walked home. Due to the extreme heat in Khartoum, there was public water provided in large clay pots called "Zeer" and there were always cups attached to them. Students as well as public members would stop by the nearest Zeer to get a cup of water before reaching home. Zeer were usually located under the shade or a tree to keep the water cool and they usually had cold water. Every Sudanese person also had them in their homes as there were no refrigerators.

When Neveen got home from school, she rested for a bit and hand-washed her uniform along with any other laundry that needed washing in the house. It was important to wash before sun down so that it could be dried by the sun in an hour or less. After laundry she would help around with house chores and help prepare lunch which was at 3 pm.

Lunch was the biggest meal of the day. Different people ate different stews, normally with a salad and water followed by a cup of tea. The base to most Sudanese food is "Dama". Dama is made of onions either fried or boiled. It was cooked until it became a paste, with tomatoes and beef and sometimes chicken. Once it was done, different kinds of vegetables or beans were used to finish the recipe. Drinking tea was huge in the Sudanese and South Sudanese culture. It was drunk in the morning and after every meal. In the evenings, people visited each other and had tea gatherings. During Ramadan season, all Muslims would gather together on the street and break their fast together in potluck style and they would pray together as well. People also drank a lot of water because of the heat. Dinner was usually at 7 pm. It was not as big of a meal unless there was a special guest visiting. Most people ate fool again for dinner. (Please view the Fool and other South Sudanese recipes at the end of the book.)

For special holidays like Eid and at Christmas there were 3 types of cookies that were made. Sudanese people made baskaweet, kaak naeem, and beautyfor cookies to celebrate these occasions. The secret recipes were passed down from generation to generation.

Groceries were done daily in Khartoum. People would take a donkey and carriage known as "Carro" to the market. They would buy everything they needed, fresh and enough for the day only. Many people did not have refrigerators. They had Zeer at home to keep water cold which was also used sometimes to make lemonade. Sudanese people were not accustomed to the idea of keeping food made today beyond today; therefore, they had no microwaves either. They ate everything fresh.

Weddings were celebrated grandly in Khartoum just as they were in South Sudan. There were minor differences as tribal cultures came into play, one of which was that Northern Sudanese married their first cousins and kept everything in the family to preserve their culture.

Neveen's religion an issue at school

Even though she was a straight A student, she was on the receiving end of a lot of bullying and discriminatory remarks by teachers and students alike. Christianity was not taught in the public schools, rather Islam was taught because it was a Muslim country. On attending the public school, Neveen had to wear hijab and was forced to study and recite the Quran. She was often called 'Kafir' or pagan. During lectures, Neveen was often made fun of because she was a

Christian. When she wanted to join the academic de-cathlon team to represent the school, she was forced to choose Islamic Studies instead of her favorite sub-ject at the time which was Science. Neveen was dis-appointed and was upset and decided that she was still going to compete and show the Muslim people that she knew about Islam even more than they did. Neveen memorized the entire Quran and read all the Ahadeeth. Her Arabic improved significantly because the teachers were training the competition team and she learned "Balagha" which was a higher level of the Arabic literature. They would make Neveen recite the Quran in front of the entire school every morning on the playground during "Taboor" which was the time when students also sang the Sudanese national an-them. Neveen got 100% in Islamic Studies in every single test and surprise quiz. The teacher would talk to the students that failed and tell them that even 'the pagan got 100% and asked them what was wrong with them.

One day, the teacher taught the class about Jihad. He said that during "Marika" or war, Mohammad fought and killed many Jews and pagans. If a Muslim kills a Jew, he or she would go to heaven and if the students killed pagans they would also go to heav-en. One of the students raised her hand and asked the teacher who would be considered a pagan. The teacher said anyone who is not Muslim is a pagan. The student replied and asked "Is Neveen a pagan?" The teacher replied with a question asking "Is she

Muslim?" The student said "No".

At that point Neveen felt that her life was in danger because there was a call to action by that lecture and she thought that her classmates were going to kill her. She pretended to have interest in converting to Islam to buy more time and to figure out her next step. The bullying increased at school and classmates were making fun of her in groups. Neveen told the principal about the danger she felt at school and that she wanted to tell her parents. Even though the principal was Muslim, she asked the Islamic studies teacher to go back to the class and address the Jihad issue. The next day, the teacher went back to the class and shared a Quranic verse about pagans. Translated, it said "to all you pagans, I don't worship what you worship and you don't worship what I worship. You have your religion and I have mine." The teacher said that Neveen was considering Islam, she should be encouraged. After that class, the bullying stopped. Students were praising Neveen for the way she recited the Quran and started to share with her about the "beauty of Islam". They would bring gifts and they told their parents about Neveen and her interest in Islam. One of the classmates said to Neveen that the Sheik and the Imam who were the leaders at the mosque heard about her achievements in school in Islamic Studies and the way she recited the Quran. They wanted to meet her and hear her recite the Quran after school. Neveen declined stating that her parents would never approve of this. The student said they would give

Neveen so much money, even to her parents. Neveen considered her family's financial situation and wanting to help, she seriously thought about it, almost convinced she was going to do it. As more Muslim students were coming with the same offer, Neveen wanted to at least tell her mother. She also realized that there was an incentive to her classmates whose efforts would be recognized if they turned her into a Muslim. Neveen did not want to stress her mother about her problems at school so she told her mother indirectly. She asked her mother if she had ever heard about Muslim people paying Christians a lot of money for converting to Muslim. Her mother quickly asked her where she had heard that. Neveen told her she just heard people talking about it. Her mother then proceeded to tell her stories about people who had done that for money and when they decided to convert back to Christianity, they were killed. That was very scary news for Neveen.

She became so afraid that she started skipping school and telling the teachers she was sick. School was no longer interesting to Neveen. All she wanted to do was stay home, do chores and help her mother. The journey was lonely and scary because Neveen was the only Christian student in the class. Soon after, the Sharia law was passed and it was mandatory for all women to wear hijab. Any woman or girl who was not in compliance with this law was whipped. All Christians were experiencing some form of pressure to convert to Islam or were having challenges with the new law. There was no one for Neveen to talk to about her issues because everyone had their own share of concerns and it was not a big problem in comparison to those who were getting executed because of their faith.

The horrible treatment of South Sudanese Christians as they were mostly Catholic was brought to Pope John Paul II. He visited Khartoum in 1993 to encourage and strengthen the faith of Sudanese Christians. The purpose of his visit was to bring a message of reconciliation to all Sudanese people regardless of religion or ethnic origin. Neveen and her family attended this service with hundreds of thousands of people from all over Sudan. After the Pope's visit, Christian women were allowed to expose their hair and wear short sleeve tops but no tank tops. Skirts had to be, below-the-knees at the very shortest, and no pants or shorts were allowed. Christians also had to wear a cross to identify themselves as Christians so they would not suffer the consequences of breaking the Sharia law. There was however, soon news about a lot of Christians disappearing in Khartoum. Some people believed it was because of the cross that identified them as Christians. The Church gave rosaries to Catholics at no cost. Some people would hide them under their clothing and some just continued wearing hijab for their safety from the law. Some wore their cross proudly and were ready to face the consequences of whatever was going to happen.

Chapter 3
Our home in Sudan

When Neveen's father's contract was over with Sudan Aid, he struggled to find a job. He was a Christian and although he spoke twenty-three languages, he did not speak Arabic fluently. Consequently, Neveen's mother had to step up and take care of the family.

The routine was to wake up at 4 am everyday with the Muslim call to people for their morning prayers. It was extremely loud and every mosque in the neighborhood would be on their microphones making the clarion call for their prayers. Neveen's mother would wake Neveen and her siblings to help her pack freshly made food to be sold in the St. Peter and Paul elementary school's cafeteria. Her mother used her family's relationship with the Catholic Church and was innovative in creating a job for herself. She worked hard and would multitask, cooking for her business and for her family and tutoring her children as they helped her.

Life became difficult for Neveen and her family. Her mother got pregnant with her brother who passed away because of medical malpractice. She was still working very hard both at home and in her business. She was also dealing with various forms of abuse from her husband's relatives, and the people who lived in the house. Resources became scarce and there were financial struggles at home. Neveen's father got a new contract in Ghana with the United Nations which necessitated his travel to Accra for work. Some of the people living in the house left and it was just Neveen, her siblings, her cousins and a couple of non-relatives. Neveen's mother continued to work hard in her business and was hustling to raise funds to not only leave the country but to also take care of her family. As her father settled in Ghana, he began preparing the paperwork for his family to join him from Egypt. When one of the people living in the house found this out, he told the Sudanese home land security that Neveen's father was a traitor to the country. He manipulated all the humanitarian assistance her father and his family provided to people as an active campaign against the north Sudanese government.

When Neveen's mother went to apply for an exit visa for her passport to travel to Egypt, her family's name was flagged. She was arrested and detained in the federal prison to be investigated about the location of her husband. Many scary and abusive tactics were used on Neveen's mother. Her children did not know her whereabouts which was very uncommon. The security agents labeled her mother as a stubborn woman and told her that she would rot in prison if she did not cooperate with them. They even produced fake marriage and birth certificates to tell her that her husband was not only a traitor to the country but to her as well. During this frightening experience, she was praying and asking God to intervene in her case. She was also a nursing mother to her new born son at the time. During her interrogation by the head of the Federal department, after his agents had aggressively interrogated her, he found out that she was one of his in-laws. That changed everything, because he knew beyond any reasonable doubt, that these allegations were not true. He did not want the rest of his team to know this fact but he did not want an innocent woman to go through what they were putting her through unnecessarily. He also did not want to show his team that he got soft with her because she was a relative by marriage. He talked to the team and told them to release her and to send one of his men to go home with her to observe the home and find any supporting evidence they could to make the charges stick.

Neveen's father had not packed heavily when he went to Ghana, therefore he left all his degrees and paperwork behind at home. Her mother's intuition told her to check her husband's luggage that was left behind as it was full of papers. The problem was that most of the documents were in English, and the agent was watching her very closely even though she had a small child that was crying all night. Neveen's mother could not speak or read English. Two of Neveen's cousins could speak English fluently so her mother asked Neveen to get her cousins to go through the bag first thing in the morning since there were no lights in the home at night. She wanted them to do it quietly without alerting the agent.Everyone at the house knew that their lives were in danger. Her mother also needed to keep the man engaged and distracted as she was extremely scared and the man only pretended to be sleeping. He was trying to entrap Neveen's mother to engage in any shady activity so he could make the charges stick or even to add to them. As always, everyone was up at 4 am. The security officer did not sleep and he kept a very close eye on Neveen's mother. He did not trust her at all.

It was shocking to find the amount of paperwork that was planted in the luggage. It did not have a lock and there were SPLA plans there that were written in English. All suspicious documents were removed from the luggage quietly.

As per the tradition of drinking tea in the morning, the fire burning stove, also known as "kanoon", was lit. All the suspicious paperwork was burnt during the tea preparation. The man was extremely intimidating and was unfriendly even while the family was being hospitable to him. He said that he had to go to the store to buy cigarettes. The store was a 5 to 7 minute walk away from the house. Everyone was all set and ready to take action. As soon as he left, all the documents were burned and a Sudanese incense was burnt as part of the cleaning routine. Tea was also made to justify the fire.

The man returned with a truck full of seven other men. Their plan was to arrest everyone at the house and find evidence. The punishment for being a traitor was execution as it was considered to be treason. The man knew what had happened and he belligerently pushed Neveen's mother out of his way. Although he was angry, he also knew that there was nothing he could do about it without evidence. He told his men that he knew that Neveen's mother could not be trusted. They aggressively searched every inch of the house to look for evidence and could not find anything. Terror was tangible as they did not care that she was a nursing woman with small children. Their desire was to arrest everyone in the house whether man or woman, young or old and take them to be executed as a punishment for their father's offense. Fear was prevalent and for the first time in her life, Neveen thought this was the end of her and her family's lives. The security agents left empty-handed but the passports were still not released. Even though nothing had been found, the passports were held for almost a month. After the men left, Neveen's mother told her, her siblings and cousins what had really happened in detail. They all prayed and thanked God for saving their lives. Because of the imminent danger, they had to leave the neighborhood for a while selling everything in the house including the doors and windows of the house. Neveen's father was not able to send money to his family from Ghana and they had no means of survival. Her mother terminated her contract with St. Peter and Paul due to her traveling arrangements and also sold a car that was in the house but her money was lost or stolen from her wallet. They moved out and lived with Neveen's grandmother. Meanwhile, Neveen's father explained everything to the UN so they started working on bringing the family to safety.

It was determined that the traveling paperwork would be easier from Egypt to Ghana and it would only be a temporary stay there until the paperwork was finished. Egypt gives visas on arrival but for Sudanese people they also needed an exit visa from Sudan. Neveen's mother still needed the passports. The house was staged so that half of the family stayed at her grandmother's house and half stayed back at the neighborhood house. At that point, there remained the trust issue because Neveen's mother was not sure who had initially reported her family. Little did she know, that someone was a relative whom she had worked hard to take care of. Even so, he did this to her and her family!

After a month and with many critical thinking ideas and strategies, the government released the passports. Neveen's mother had to borrow money and prepare to secretly travel to Egypt. Neveen's grandmother and aunties on her mother's side gave up their assets to make sure that the family had enough money in Egypt as they heard stories that life was not that easy in Egypt. Neveen's mother did not want her family to travel by air to alert the Sudanese Homeland Security in Khartoum so they took the train to a city in the north Sudan called Wadi Halfa. They traveled discretely and left the house furnished. Everything was normal as if they were coming back in the evening but that was the last day that Neveen spent in Sudan. They had been granted an exit visa. From Wadi Halfa they then took a boat to Aswan, in South Egypt. Their visa was granted and their lives changed instantly, beginning with taking the train from Aswan to Cairo.

Chapter 4

Refugee in Egypt

E
gypt is another one of the most alluring countries in the world. It is located north of Sudan in northeast Africa. Tourists come every day from all over the world to see one of the seven wonders of the ancient world, the pyramid of Giza. It has a very rich history and boasts many side tourist attractions. The pyramid of Giza was humanly constructed from block stone and is the only one left standing.

Beauty from the Ashes of War

Cairo is the capital of Egypt. It became overpopulated quickly at that time due to tourism and refugees, especially the South Sudanese looking for resettlement. It was easy to seek refuge in Egypt for the Sudanese and South Sudanese people because the Arabic dialogue is easy to pick up and understand. The first language in Sudan and Egypt is Arabic. There are many dialogues of Arabic and they often sound like different languages. For example English is spoken in the UK, North America, some parts of Africa and the Caribbean. Patois (an English-based Creole language), pidgin, North American and European English dialogues are not the same. The same is true for Arabic.

Egyptians do not consider themselves to be Africans. They will tell you that they are just Egyptians. Neveen's first impression about Egypt was shock. When the boat took her and her family from Wadi Halfa to Aswan, she was very surprised to learn that the Egyptian people there are black and look exactly like Sudanese people. Their skin was very dark and their hair was dark brown. The only difference was their Egyptian accent and straighter hair almost like the Sri Lankans. It was quite fascinating for Neveen. This was the first time that someone called her "Samara" and "hunga bonga". Neveen understood Samara which means "dark skin" but till this day she has no idea what hunga bonga means. At the beginning she thought they were welcoming her because they were laughing and walking away. Hunga bonga is not an

Beauty from the Ashes of War

Arabic word. It is a derogatory term that black people are called when they visit Egypt. The sad part is that even the dark-skinned Egyptians used those terms when talking to each other. It was so confusing! Neveen thought that Egyptians had white skin and she wanted to know why the ones she met in Aswan were black and reminded her of Sudanese people.

History of Aswan- Kingdom of Kush

The kingdom of Kush was the African region along the River Nile between Aswan, Egypt and Khartoum, Sudan. It was an ancient kingdom in Nubia and was home of Africa's earliest kingdoms. Ancient Egyptians went to Sudan to mine copper. Monuments and statues were made from the Sudanese copper in modern Egypt and Sudan where rulers build cities, temples and royal pyramids. It was also known for its rich deposits of gold and luxury products. As conflicts around the borders continued, even until today, the Nubians who lived in that region were divided into what are known as Egypt and Sudan today.

Neveen's first impression of Cairo was that everything was very fast. When she got off the train with her family, it was like a scene from a movie. Everything was extremely different. People bumping into each other as they walked; wherever one looked, people were packed together. They were welcoming at the train station and were very friendly and funny. There were cabs everywhere at the station, with direct and intense competition for passenger pick-ups. If a cab driver did not know how to talk to customers and entice them with deals, he would not have any customers. Women did not drive cabs, at least Neveen never saw any.

Egyptians were very good in business and they knew how to quickly adapt to the customers' style and manner of communication to seal a deal. They liked to tell jokes and laugh a lot whether it was with you or at you. They were insensitive to people's feelings, only focusing on their hustle. They often spoke in rude aggressive manners and swore a lot, regardless of age. People did not take much offense to this manner of communication because they would swear back or make fun of each other. It was shocking for Neveen to hear these kinds of conversation because no one spoke in such a manner in Sudan or South Sudan.

At the beginning, the insults were very personal because they were directed at Neveen when she conversed with Egyptians. She would often cry and get teased. The Egyptian people also expected tips for everything that they did including small favors or good manners such as opening the door for someone. Bribing people was a very common practice. It was exercised openly. To receive good service everyone had to give tips or bribes which the Egyptians called "Bakhshish".

Beauty from the Ashes of War

In Sudan and South Sudan people helped each other out because they needed the help. In Egypt, people demanded tips and bribes on top of their paid services or they would follow it up with some type of insult. When at times Neveen did not factor the bribe into the cost of something, she was insulted, spat at or was told to go back to her country.

Profanity was used so often in conversations and people's mothers were often insulted as part of the swearing. In North America, this type of insult and swearing could land someone dead on the spot but in Egypt they were used daily by everyone. Neveen and her family brought a lot of wearable gold to Egypt as assets given to them by her grandmother and aunties, to be liquidated in Egypt. They had necklaces, rings, bracelets, and watches. Egyptians loved Sudanese gold. Gold was as good as cash in those days and Egyptians paid more money for it. Neveen's mother also had Kuwaiti dinar which had the highest currency exchange in Egypt, even higher than the British pound. Coming to Egypt, her mother knew that the Egyptian pound was stronger than the Sudanese pound but she did not know that the dinar was as strong as it was.

On first arriving, they eventually entered a cab and Neveen's mother asked the cab driver to help her and her family get a hotel in Cairo until they could meet up with Neveen's aunt. The driver was acting incredibly nice. He told her mother not to worry, that Egypt is the mother of all nations and that Egyptians love seeing people come from all over the world to visit their country. He also said that Egypt and Sudan are the same people so "we are relatives by blood". It was a popular saying in Egypt at the time.

He dropped them off at a hotel that looked nice from the outside but when they got into the room, it turned out to be disgusting, putting it mildly! There were huge cockroaches crawling everywhere.

Not only did the cab driver bring them to the sub-standard accommodations but he swindled Neveen's mother and stole her dinar. He told her the cost of the cab ride was "way more than what he was charging but since she was new to Egypt and she was like a relative he would let it go". When Neveen's mother went to the bank, she realized that the cab driver had overcharged her by more than 10,000%. This was the first time that the family had left Sudan and dealt with a new currency. Also coming from a background where people would never have done something like that, the family felt incredibly naive. That was the first rip off experience of many in Egypt. They only stayed in the hotel for one night before getting reunited with the aunt.

The family learned from the cab experience that it was very important to be street smart when it came to dealing with Egyptians. The culture was to assume everyone is there to rip you off and it is your job to find out how and what you can do about it. Distrust was a huge issue in Egypt. It was encountered everywhere especially with law enforcement. One needed larger bribes for police officers as they had the power to send people back to Sudan. They often abused their power because of their knowledge of this information.

Going to the hospital for any reason was the biggest risk any South Sudanese person could take because of human trafficking. They knew that most Sudanese people could not afford to pay for medical care so they would take their organs and sell them in the black market for millions of dollars. South Sudanese people have very strong genes and there was high demand for their organs. Neveen and her family avoided going to the hospital for any reason and used natural remedies when they were sick. Many Sudanese and South Sudanese people who went to the hospital for appendix surgeries ended up with huge scars and a missing kidney! There was no one to advocate for them or to help them out except the churches.

There were three different churches in Cairo that were assisting South Sudanese people: Sacred Heart Catholic Church, Manshiat Sadr Anglican Church and Amberwest Orthodox Church. Sacred Heart Catholic Church provided South Sudanese refugees a place to gather as a community to pray and be active members. There was an elementary and intermediate school in the church called St. Charles Lwanga Centre

For Basic Education that was taught by South Sudanese teachers and guidance counselors. In addition, there was a cafeteria and restaurant that sold South Sudanese food. All family and cultural celebrations were performed at the church. The annual Christmas play was performed by South Sudanese church members of different ages. There was a South Sudanese basketball team that only played against each other as they were divided into groups. The church also sent the South Sudanese youth to a summer vacation in Alexandria. Often, a container full of food, mainly rice and lentils was distributed to families to feed off of and to help with groceries. Another container also often brought used clothing for South Sudanese refugees in Egypt. A lot of aid was provided for South Sudanese church members and they were excited and looked forward to the aids.

At Manshiat Sadr, South Sudanese people were provided with another community avenue where they could congregate, pray and receive aids. It was a small, new church. Neveen and her family were one of the first members of the church and helped establish the church in the South Sudanese community. Neveen was in the choir along with one of her cousins. They would meditate on the Word and try to turn it into songs. There were weekly overnights of prayers at the church and similar food and clothing aid was provided for church members.

Amberwest Orthodox Church was a church that

had services monthly for South Sudanese people. During service, they would sing, share the Word and pray. At the end of service, every single attendee of the service was given money, including children. The money was between five to twenty Egyptian pounds. South Sudanese people would come with their families and engage in the services. They also provided aid of food and clothing.

Neveen and her family attended all three churches and were grateful to all the assistance that these churches provided them. Neveen's mother always taught her and her siblings to work hard and to find a way around every difficult situation they had. She was so innovative and strong. Focusing on her strength, she came up with an idea of South Sudanese food pick-up and delivery. She realized that she could not get a contract anywhere so she created a job for herself and her kids. She made some of the most delicious Sudanese and South Sudanese food and the demand quickly grew. She would wake up at 4 am as usual and prepare all the fresh food for both pick-up and delivery.

Neveen and her family lived in Madinat Nasr in Al Hay El Sabieh. It was a suburban neighborhood that was centrally located near many amenities including Neveen's favourite grocery store Misr Wel Sudan or Egypt and Sudan. This super market was high end and had fresh and delicious Egyptian and Sudanese food. Neveen loved buying lunch meat and desserts from there. She attended Al Sayeda Khadija Intermediate School in Egypt. Neveen's parents did not want her to attend St. Charles Lwanga Center For Basic Education school because it was not well structured and they were not sure if the school's credentials would be recognized. Neveen had her credentials from Sudan and although the Egyptian schools recognized them, she repeated grade 3 intermediate school since she had not completed it due to all that happened when she and her family had to escape Sudan. Al Sayeda Khadija was a big school. Students would form lines in the morning and sing the national anthem in the middle of the school's playground similar to Sudan. Announcements would be made and a uniformed march to class would follow singing of the national anthem.. All subjects were taught every day.

When it came to religion class, all the Muslim students remained in class while the Christian students had a Christian class separately. It was a breath of fresh air for Neveen. She was not the only Christian student in the school. There was a group of almost 10 students who were Christian Orthodox. Even though they were Egyptians and had a light complexion, they were also bullied just as badly as Neveen for their religion. The school was a public school and was predominantly Muslim. There was a zoning restriction and Al Sayeda Khadija was the only school in Neveen's zone.

Neveen met many people in Egypt named Neveen.

Beauty from the Ashes of War

It was a popular Egyptian name. She was able to make new friends who would also defend her when other Egyptian kids would make fun of her because of her skin tone or the way she looked. Egyptian kids did not understand diversity nor were they open to anything that was not Egyptian. They saw themselves better than the Arabs and definitely better than Africans because they did not consider themselves Africans. They had a lot of love and hate for America. They loved the American dollars and would say "mama Amrica dollaratha be teshtarika." It means "mother America its dollars can purchase you." They also liked the American fashion style but hated their culture and invasion into everyone's problems.

Egyptians loved rhyming and telling jokes. When South Sudanese people would walk down the street, Egyptians would start provoking them by calling them blacky, hunga bonga or any other derogatory term and ask them what have they done to themselves or ask each other when women passed by if it was their hair or not. Some of them would run and take a wig off of a black South Sudanese woman's head and they would all laugh hysterically. They would either pass the wig to each other, throw it on the ground or into the garbage and call the woman an animal. When South Sudanese people would not respond to their behavior, they would spit at them, or throw garbage, dirty water, rotten food or any disgusting thing that they could find. They would do the same to strangers on the street who were just minding their own business.

They would offer South Sudanese refugees the worst jobs at the lowest pay and would not even pay sometimes. When purchasing goods, Egyptians would always over charge and offer the worst possible products to South Sudanese people. They would make statements around black people, especially Sudanese people, that their country was getting dirty because of all the garbage that was coming from the South in reference to the people. Whenever Neveen and her friends got together at church, they often talked about horrible acts that were committed by Egyptians against them or other South Sudanese people in the community. The youth were most affected by the excessive bullying. There were a couple of solutions that were suggested among the youth. There were groups that wanted to come up with ideas to avoid the bullying and groups that were fed up and wanted to respond to it with violence. One of the strategies that the young South Sudanese girls were using was skin bleaching.

The skin is the largest organ in the body. It protects the body with its multi-layered and water-resistant barrier. Before discussing skin bleaching issues in the South Sudanese community in Egypt, Neveen wants to share important information about the skin, its types and conditions to help the reader(s) understand the bleaching effect on the skin.

Beauty from the Ashes of War

Healthy skin is slightly acidic with a pH of 4.5 to 5.6. Regardless of ethnic background, every person has different skin types and conditions. There are four different skin types: normal, dry, oily and combination.

Normal Skin

Normal or young skin is well balanced in oil and moisture. It is not prone to sensitivity. The skin is young but as it ages, it can become dry.

Characteristics of normal skin
- fine pores
- good blood circulations
- soft and smooth texture
- fresh, clear, even and rosy in color
- glows from within
- has no blemishes
- radiant complexion
- T-zone is a little oily
- subtle and luminous
- good moisture balance

Dry Skin

Dry skin is a skin type where the sebaceous glands produce less oil than the normal skin type. It requires moisturizing and hydrating to build protection for the skin against natural and artificial environments. There are various degrees of skin dryness to this skin type. It is constantly losing moisture. Skin can crack, get irritated, become itchy or inflamed. It is caused or becomes worse because of genes, aging, hormonal changes, weather, ultraviolet radiation from tanning, artificial heat, long hot baths and showers, medication and ingredients in cosmetic products

Characteristics of dry skin
- red, tight and flaky
- sensitive
- matte in texture
- possible itchiness
- rough and blotchy
- low skin elasticity and collagen
    - Hyper pigmentation and puffiness
- dehydrated
- more visible lines and wrinkles

Oily Skin

Oily skin is a skin type where the sebaceous glands over produce oil. It is passed down genetically. It can occur due to hormone changes and imbalances, medication, stress or through makeup products that irritate the skin. Oiliness varies as the weather changes throughout the year. It is caused or becomes worse because of puberty or other hormonal imbalances, stress, heat or excessive humidity.

Characteristics of oily skin
- Large pores
- glossy and shiny in appearance
- thicker in texture
- invisible blood vessels
- prone to blackheads and whiteheads
- Problematic and dehydrated
- susceptible to skin allergies
- Ages very well
- high elasticity

Combination Skin

Combination skin is a skin type that has both dry and oily patches

Characteristics of combination skin
- partly dry and partly oily
- oily T-zone (forehead, nose and chin)
- normal to dry cheeks
- large pores in T-zone with some impurities
- partially shiny
- common skin-type in colder areas

Unlike skin types, skin conditions can vary throughout a human life cycle. There are many factors that influence skin conditions including climate, pollution, medication, stress, hereditary factors, sweat, and cosmetic products that a person uses. In addition to the conditions characterized per skin type, some of the most common skin conditions include signs of aging, skin tone, and skin sensitivity. Other conditions include dehydration, hyper-pigmentation, broken capillaries and skin disorders.

Signs of aging

All skin ages as a person is gets older regardless of the skin type. Oily or acne prone skin become drier post-puberty as well as normal skin. As the skin ages it typically becomes drier and that is the reason why moisturizing and hydrating the skin is so important. An aging skin loses its texture, volume and density. Due to loss of moisture and hydration, it becomes wrinkled and fine lines become visible in appearance. Change in pigmentation also occurs. As one looks in the mirror everyday it is important to notice these visible signs of aging and start addressing them right away. Drinking plenty of water, eating a healthy diet, exercising and using a skincare routine that is appropriate for the current skin type will slow down aging before using more intensive solutions such as cosmetic surgeries. Neveen Dominic Cosmetics™ has a dermatologist formulated skincare line that addresses visible signs of aging including its age reversal system. Visit their website, www.neveendominic.com, to learn more.

Skin tone

Skin tone and ethnicity influence the way skin reacts to the sun, pigmentation disorders, irritation, inflammation and other external forces. Basic skin tone is determined by the distribution of melanin and skin texture. The higher the density the more intense the skin tone is. Redness is helpful in measuring skin conditions. It provides information about dehydration and circulation which helps identify conditions such as rosacea.

Sensitivity

Sensitive skin is a skin that is easily irritated. It is more reactive to products than normal skin. Sensitive skin is red, dry, itchy, stingy and burning. It is extremely important to find out what the skin is allergic to or sensitive to and to avoid the triggers. Although there are many reasons that cause the skin to be sensitive, it is often due to reactions to skin care products, both natural and synthetic.

Skin bleaching

Skin bleaching is a cosmetic depigmentation skin treatment used to remove dark spots caused by aging, blemishes, disease, hormone changes and sun damage. It was intended to correct skin conditions and bring the skin back to its original state, not to be used all over the body to modify its genetic tone. Skin bleaching or lightening is the process in which chemicals are used to reduce melanin in the skin and make it appear lighter. Dermatologists recommend the use of bleaching creams for two to three months and not for a life time. The dangers of using skin bleaching products are the ingredients in them such as hydroquinone, kojic acid, retinoids, botanical and tropical corticosteroids. Applying these products all over the body is very risky because the skin type and condition of the face is not the same as the different parts of the body. It is extremely risky also because the active ingredient in most skin lighteners is mercury which is a poison. Mercury is a toxic agent that causes serious psychiatric, neurological, and kidney problems. Pregnant women who use skin bleaching can pass down the mercury to their unborn child which can cause still birth. Because there are different types and conditions of skin, bleaching products affect people differently. In some cases, adverse reactions include severe skin burn and facial dis-figuration.

South Sudanese people during the war were not focusing on education. Safety was the number one priority. Also, in Egypt there were not many computers at the time anywhere and no one taught the youth about the importance of researching products before using them on the skin. Parents were concerned about providing the basic necessities of life for their families to survive and teachers were doing their best at St. Charles Lwanga Center For Basic Education to keep

South Sudanese students busy with studying important subjects like Math, English, Arabic and Science. There was no library or computers accessible to people. South Sudanese girls knew that Egyptians treated lighter-skinned Sudanese girls like the girls from northern Sudan much better that the South Sudanese girls because of their light complexion.

Skin bleaching quickly became a trend and everyone was working hard to save money to bleach their skin. Men, women and even children were bleaching their skin to avoid being targeted on the streets by Egyptians. Neveen also considered doing the same thing.

People who could not afford to bleach their skin started to mix different household chemical products such as baking soda mixed with other chemicals to apply on their skin. Some took baths with bleached water to wash the black off themselves as they couldn't afford it. Purchasing bleaching products which were in very high demand was so expensive that it became a choice between shelter or cream. Even then it was not enough for the entire body so people only bleached their faces as a starting point. People who successfully bleached their skin were congratulated and were viewed as celebrities in the South Sudanese community and were more appreciated by Egyptians. Those who were in the process were bullied more severely than those who didn't use bleach. Egyptians would walk up to them and ask them what they have done to themselves. Sometimes they would smack people on the back of their heads with their hand and it was what they called "Affah."

One day Neveen was playing basketball with one of her coaches who had successfully bleached her skin. They were passing the ball to her and she missed it and the ball touched her face. The area where the ball hit looked like a facial explosion to Neveen. The game was stopped and the coach had to go to the hospital for treatment. It was so traumatizing. Right then, Neveen knew that bleaching her skin was not an option, even as a means for her to reduce bullying by Egyptians.

The bullying was more towards the youth but elderly South Sudanese were bullied too. Bleach was extremely harsh on mature skin so some elderly people had to consider other strategies to protect themselves. South Sudanese people were going through mental, emotional and even physical abuse by Egyptians. Some people were even killed just because they were dark. The darker the person was, the more he or she was hated. The situation was serious and everyone was experiencing the discrimination, both men and women, young and old. The churches were aware of it and were working hard with the South Sudanese Community to find solutions. They taught the community to ignore it and let the words go in one ear and out the other. There was nothing that could be done about the physical attacks except to respond with self-defense which was often ruled in favor of the Egyptian offender(s).

Youth responding to violence

The South Sudanese youth were getting tired of the bullying which continued to escalate to the point that Egyptians would physically attack South Sudanese people regardless of age and fight them. They would tell them to go back to their country, throw acid at people's faces and other demonstrations of hate. The churches and many organizations tried to interfere but the Egyptians were not listening. Some even condemned the churches and asked them to focus on poor Egyptians that were living in impoverished communities who were in need of what they were giving to South Sudanese people.

The violence continued to intensify as South Sudanese people started to form groups to defend themselves and others against Egyptians. There was a lot of fear in the South Sudanese community. People did not go out much. Attendance at church even reduced because Egyptian groups knew where South Sudanese people congregated and they were often attacked after those events. Human trafficking and violence in the community increased. South Sudanese people were losing their lives and becoming disabled at odd jobs like maid services with reports of people falling off balconies or getting poisoned at work by their Egyptian employers. Working in public places like coffee shops or restaurants was hazardous due to the nature of the job description and attacks at work by Egyptians. Many young South Sudanese girls were raped as they went to school or church. There was also a terrorist group called Al Irhabi that was formed during that time so the violence was getting out of control. The Egyptian government, churches and humanitarian organizations including United Nations knew about the inhumane treatments of the South Sudanese people in Egypt. Humanitarian aid was urgently needed to rescue South Sudanese refugees as it was war all over again but in a different country.

Beauty from the Ashes of War

Chapter 5
Basketball

Basketball was and is Neveen's favourite sport. She was introduced to the sport in Egypt when she was fifteen and she fell totally in love with it. The St. Charles Lwanga Center For Basic Education had a basketball team. Neveen could not be a part of it because she did not attend the school. To her joy there was however a South Sudanese youth basketball team that was formed and she was able to join it. Students from St. Charles Lwanga Center For Basic Education school were also part of the team.

Beauty from the Ashes of War

Neveen was super excited to connect with more South Sudanese kids from that school and she also learned that there was a boys group that was formed. Both boys and girls would warm up during practice as one team. After warm up, the girls and boys groups would be divided and they would practice separately in each half of the court. Neveen was the captain of the girls' team. She would practice every day, as being the captain, she got to keep the ball. She loved the game passionately, working out every day, practicing her dribbling at home and everywhere, driving everyone crazy!

Neveen loved running errands for her mother to the store so she could take her basketball with her and dribble peacefully there and back. Neveen wanted to be the very best possible in that game. She used to play with boys because they were stronger and better which made her skills better. Boys would cheer so much when Neveen used moves they had taught her when she was playing with them and they would brag that they taught her the moves. She became closer to boys and they loved her passion for the game. Her routine was to find out where practice was as locations often changed due to safety and availability. She always showed up half an hour to an hour early to practice by herself and with the boys prior to regular practise. When the coaches came she often lead the warm up as captains and coaches were the only ones who could lead them. The girls and boys divided for practice and the full court was used after practice for a girls' game followed by a boys' game. The game was Neveen's favourite part of the practice. Basketball was everything to her and it brought her so much joy. The boys' team often got together and they watched previously-recorded, borrowed NBA basketball game tapes.

Neveen loved hanging out with the boys because they taught her the game in more detail and they explained a lot to her. She was fascinated by the Chicago Bulls and in particular Michael Jordan. She used to dream about him day and night and wanted to be just like him. She wasn't allowed to borrow the tapes as watching the tape was an event and it was only the coach who had them and was responsible for them. The more she heard about Michael Jordan's life, the more excited she got about basketball. He was her first role model and she was totally crazy about him. This was the first time also that Neveen thought of America as a cool place. She always knew that one day she and her family were going to go back to South Sudan but she never thought that she would want to see outside of Egypt and Sudan. This was the best memory that Neveen has of her refugee journey in Egypt.

Neveen's mother was not a fan of Neveen's new found love, basketball. She totally misunderstood Neveen's passion for the game as being passionate-about boys. This used to upset Neveen and offended her because she never understood why her mother would have those "disgusting" ideas about her. The subject would irritate Neveen as she wasn't thinking about boys at all until her mother negatively introduced the idea of boys to her.

During this period of her life, they did not have a good relationship, and Neveen developed a form of resentment for her mother because of it. Her mother would report Neveen to her father because every time they were at church, Neveen would always be talking to boys instead of girls and she would be so excited. She often talked to them about the game and the following week's practice. Her mother would often embarrass her by either giving her dirty looks from across the room or telling her they had to go. At times she would even discipline her in public. Neveen was also not contributing much to chores at the house at this time since she was continuously going to basketball practice. Sometimes she would come home and would find her mother at the bus stop, agitated because she was late. No matter how much Neveen tried to explain to her that practice went on longer than the schedule and her passion was only for basketball, she did not seem to be understanding or supportive.

Basketball season ended and although Neveen wanted to continue playing, there were no opportunities available except for the times she went and played at church with the boys. She considered herself one of them. It could even be said she was a real tomboy.

Luckily for Neveen the church was sending the youth for a summer vacation to Alexandria. Neveen had missed a trip to Luxor before with her father and she wanted to see somewhere else other than Cairo. Neveen had never been on vacation in her entire life. She did not know what to expect but she was happy that the boys were going to be there and there would be an opportunity to play basketball.

Neveen signed up to go to the camp and she asked her father who was always busy talking about politics and always wanted to get rid of her so he could go back to what he was doing. Neveen always asked her father for things that she needed a yes answer to, such as this trip. She also knew exactly what to tell him when he wanted to think about it or ask her mother. She told him that the trip was organized by the Catholic Church and positioned it more as a retreat to build her faith. No South Sudanese Catholic parent would say no to that. Some parents had conflicting opinions about this trip and Neveen did not want her father to be manipulated by those parents. She got the trip leader to talk to her father, he approved it, and she asked him if they could leave right away so that he would not talk to anyone else besides the leader. They left and took the bus home. The thought of not having her parents, especially her mother breathing down her neck every single day was very exciting to Neveen. When they got home, her mother wanted to ask so many questions and wanted to call around about it. Her father told her that he had signed the papers and Neveen was leaving right away. He made Neveen's mother comfortable about the trip and for the first time ever her mother was supportive of the trip activity, particularly because Neveen was going with 2 of her cousins. All the youth were excited and everyone in the community was talking about the three day trip.

Neveen's mother was not good at doing hair. She braided Neveen's hair in big single braids with extensions as she was concerned about the tomboy look that Neveen had. She was worried that no one would be interested in her daughter for marriage if she continued to look boyish. Neveen did not care much about that because she was not thinking about marriage or boys and found those conversations uncomfortable and highly repulsive. Her mother did not know how to talk to Neveen about sex. Every time she tried Neveen would rather die than hear her broach the subject. Her mother would tell her that if she opened her legs to a boy or if boys saw her naked body she would have HIV or get pregnant. Neveen did not know what her mother was talking about and she often wondered why in God's name would someone want to get naked other than taking a shower. Neveen would often cry after these conversations and she believed that her mother hated her because she did not know why she wanted to keep talking about 'that' and accuse her of things that she was not even thinking about.

The trip was a life-changing event for Neveen. When they got to the summer camp, there was a lot of good food, games and activities that Neveen had never been engaged in before. She loved everything about it. Alexandria was so beautiful and she had so many first time life experiences there. The Egyptian people were way nicer there than the ones from Cairo.

Neveen had never been to the beach before. It was her first time. She did not know how to swim and the beach was full of people from all over the world, including many Egyptians. It was outside of her comfort zone. Most people could swim but Neveen. One of the camp members was trying to teach Neveen how to swim and asked her to dip her head in the water. Neveen did and it was a bit scary. As Neveen continued to try, her braid extensions got heavy because of the water since they were made of a fiber material. Soon, they started falling off her hair. This turned out to be so embarrassing because not only did Neveen notice them but everyone else at the beach did too. People started laughing and kids passed her braids around to each other like a ball. The Egyptians were asking if it was Neveen's real hair or not. Neveen quickly got out of the water crying, wanting desperately to go home.

Her cousins and the camp counselors talked to her and the immediate solution was for her to wear a scarf to cover her head. Going home to Cairo was not possible because it was day one of the camp and Cairo was three hours away. Neveen did not participate in any other activities that afternoon.

Some of the other girls were also being teased and asked if their hair was real by Egyptian outsiders. Neveen felt so bad about that experience that she took out all her braids when they got to the camp. Some of the girls were upset with Neveen for embarrassing everyone while others comforted her.

None of the boys wanted to play basketball. All they wanted to do was chase girls at the camp and engage in inappropriate behaviour like kissing and hugging and finding places where they could make out with the girls. Neveen and her cousins were shocked and stayed in groups that were focused on singing and praising God. Neveen really wanted to be alone because she could not fit in with most of the groups. Day one was depressing and lonely.

The following days got better and the experience was good over all. Her cousin was always there with Neveen and they talked a lot, realizing that they needed to change. They needed liberation and breaking out of their shells. They tried their best to learn from everyone at the camp, not wanting to be so naive and sheltered. They also promised to never tell Neveen's parents about all that had transpired at the camp so they would not get punished.

After the camp Neveen had a complete mindset change. She started to be attracted to boys and she realized that basketball was not all that boys liked. She wanted to be viewed as attractive and she knew that it started with hair.

Neveen could do other people's braids but could not do her own. Braids were expensive to get done and her parents could not afford to by her nicer extensions so she had to be very creative. She and her cousin decided that they would put their money together and buy a better quality hair and they would share it and take turns braiding their hair with it. Neveen started braiding her hair and exploring with different hairstyles and scarves. She also started to fade a little from the tomboy look.

As South Sudanese people were looking at magazines and music videos from America, hairstyles and fashion became competitive, coupled with skin bleaching. Some people were getting their relatives and friends from the US to send them human hair and they would rent it to people to braid their hair with it for 2 months at a time. They would wash them after each use and rent or sell them at reduced prices. The more they were used the cheaper they were.

Even though the kind of hair that Neveen used to do her hair was not of high quality, she always knew how to braid and put it together so that people would ask "Who did your hair?" or "How did you do it?" Neveen's primary objective was to never let the beach experience happen again. She would spend days doing her hair and she made sure that every braid was as perfect as it could be.

There was a never-ending challenge and pressure about image for Neveen. Some girls discovered doctors outside Cairo and heard of countries that would give injections that would grow the hair and permanently change skin tone to even white. They were showing many African-American celebrities who apparently did that. All this while, Neveen's relationship with her mother was going downhill. She was concerned about Neveen and did not want anything bad to happen to her. All the new exciting changes for Neveen were leaving her mother so concerned. She was constantly worried and going through Neveen's things to find information on what she and her cousins were up to. There was no trust because Neveen hid everything from her and her mother was constantly accusing her and calling her names. All that her mother wanted her to do was house chores and go to church. There were even a lot of restrictions on what was allowed at church.

Neveen hated life because she had nothing to look forward to. Things were bad everywhere; at home, school and in the community. She started contemplating suicide. She felt like an orphan in her own father's house.

Through Neveen's inner searching, she remembered that during one of the services, a scripture was shared saying that God is a father to the fatherless.

She started a new relationship with the idea of that father because her father was too busy with politics and her mother was making her life a living hell. She started praying to this Father and asked for peace from Him in every area of her life. She wanted Him to stop the bullying and all the negative experiences in her life. She made a deal with Him. The deal was if He would stop all the pain and hurt, she would give Him all the glory and credit for everything. Neveen felt good every time she spoke to God about things and He made them better. He became a good friend to her and whenever she had no one to talk to, or needed a miracle, He made it happen. She saw Him as a good, imaginary father.

Chapter 6

The United Nations Aid

The violence and terror continued to increase in Egypt. Medical malpractice and human trafficking cases also significantly increased. South Sudanese people went missing regularly. It was war all over again and the target was South Sudanese people. Integrating into the Egyptian society became a huge risk that any South Sudanese person could take so they stayed segregated. Trips to the grocery stores were minimized. People would purchase imported groceries from Sudan from each other's homes and they would also rely on the aids from churches. There was news about the Egyptian beef being mixed with human meat, especially ground beef. A lot of people were getting sick. Egypt was not advanced in technology or forensic science, the food was not inspected regularly and allegations were not often investigated. It was hard to get justice in most cases.

The black market and underground economy continued to grow as the population of South Sudanese people continued to increase in Egypt. There was also news of human kidneys being sold in the black market for millions of US dollars because they were in very high demand. South Sudanese genes were considered strong because the people ate everything fresh and their food was organic. They did not get sick often, so they were viewed as high quality in the black market. Egyptian Christians also went missing regularly. The church continued to warn people and encouraged them to stick together. South Sudanese people started to go to church in groups and had whistles to blow. People started to move closer to each other and looked out for each other as they did back in South Sudan.

Reports of atrocities, slavery and maltreatment of South Sudanese people in Egypt went to the United Nations. They already had hundreds of thousands of cases in Sudan. The UN could not rescue South Sudanese people from the war in South Sudan and the north Sudanese government would not cooperate with them to assist South Sudanese people living in Khartoum or anywhere else.

In Egypt the situation was urgent and desperate. In Sudan people were being kidnapped and put into slavery. In Ethiopia and Kenya, South Sudanese people were also going through difficult situations and different forms of maltreatment. People checked with other South Sudanese people living in different countries to see if the situation was any better for them in the country they were living in. Some South Sudanese people moved to Asian countries like China and India but reported similar abusive situations and some were even worse than Egypt. South Sudanese people felt stuck and decided that the "devil they knew was better than the saint they did not know!!"

Neveen and her friends were all living in a state of fear. They did not see each other often except occasionally at church. They spoke on the phone and stayed home most of the time to avoid getting raped or kidnapped. Neveen was emotionally frustrated and had nothing to look forward to. She loved and appreciated her family very much and could not bear the thought of anything evil happening to them.

As reports were coming to the UN from all over the world about South Sudanese people and their vulnerability to slavery and abuse, they opened immigration doors to Western world countries, particularly North America and Australia. South Sudanese refugees had a life changing opportunity through the United Nations to have a new home where there were more Christians and less abuse. The news was like heaven itself opening and God rescuing the people of South Sudan. The news was not openly announced and everyone in the community did not know about it at first. People just did not see each other and were wondering if they were kidnapped. As they reached their new homes, they started reporting good news to the rest of the refugees in Egypt. The community was happy for them and wanted to know how they too could get out of their situation.

When Neveen's mother found out about the immigration opportunity, she figured out how to apply. She put her family's case together and submitted her application to the UN to resettle in North America. She thought about it from a business perspective as the family had no relatives or friends in Canada or the United States. This was by far the highest risk but the family had nothing to lose. The UN already heard Neveen's mother's case from when she was in Sudan. The interview process was quick. The UN assessed the family's education, experience and their likelihood of surviving in North America. Neveen's father was educated and had a lot of work experience. He also spoke English and French and could help his family learn the language as they only spoke Arabic. The medical tests came out well and they had no issues with security clearance during their stay in Egypt. The family fasted and prayed every day and

Beauty from the Ashes of War

relied on God for making this miracle happen. It was an emotional roller coaster because it was exciting and scary at the same time.

The results came in positively and Neveen and her family were given permanent residency to both Canada and the United States. For the US, her family were offered a 3 year work contract for their father, a two story house and a family car. For Canada, they were offered a two story house and government financial support until they got jobs. This was the happiest news that the family had received in a very long time. The only problem that they had was to decide which one of the two countries they should choose. It was a very difficult choice. The UN was giving all refugees a loan to buy their tickets with interest and they would have to pay it back as soon as they got to their destinations. Neveen's family were a little relieved to know that they did not have to come up with all the money upfront as it was extremely expensive considering they were a family of eight.

Neveen's mother thought that America was better because the dollar was stronger and the opportunities to hustle and make a lot of money were all there. She was thinking about the American dream and the financial resources for the family. There were also a lot of black people in America and it would not be that big of a shock. She also thought about guns and violence. Neveen and her siblings were all in their early teenage years at the time. She was concerned about puberty, sex, drugs and alcohol. Many people told her horror stories about teenage kids going to America and not being able to positively deal with the American culture. They got disrespectful to their parents and called the police on them. Some joined gangs and sold drugs. The rate of teenage pregnancy was alarming. The news also reported many stories about black people experiencing injustice and going to prison so she backed out of that choice. Neveen was so excited and wanted her family to choose the US. Some of her friends were emigrating to the States, but she was thinking mostly about basketball and the opportunity of meeting Michael Jordan. She wanted to be an NBA player and she could not wait. She just kept on dreaming about her success in basketball and how proud her coaches and teammates would be when they started watching her games on tapes from America. She wanted everyone to be proud and wanted to inspire other South Sudanese kids to play basketball. The offer was to move to New York so that her father could work for the UN and her mother would start her own business and make a lot of money. It made it so much sweeter for Neveen as she used to listen to rap music. She learned about Brooklyn when she heard singers like Foxy Brown rap about it. Everyone talked so highly about New York. Neveen was also thinking about the American dream and making it as the first South Sudanese girl in the NBA.

Neveen's mother thought that Canada was calm and a good place to raise children. Everyone was

Beauty from the Ashes of War

speaking positively about it except making money was not easy in Canada and the Canadian dollar was weaker than the US dollar. Her mother was concerned about money conversion from the Canadian currency to Egyptian pounds as Egyptians preferred US currency and offered better exchange rates for it. Neveen's mother was a little relieved because the government supported refugees as newcomers to Canada. She figured that it was a good start and she would figure something else out when she got to the land. Neveen did not want her family to choose Canada. None of her friends were going there plus they made fun of the place and said that Canadians lived in igloos. They also described living in Canada like living in a refrigerator. The idea of going to Canada was so depressing to Neveen. She prayed that God should make her parents choose America but in the end they chose Canada. Neveen was not happy about this choice. She was also sad that her cousin could not travel with them and she had to leave all her friends behind. Her cousin had to stay with another relative who was helping her as Neveen's father was working on her papers after Neveen and her family left. Her cousin later joined them.

Neveen's parents asked her and her siblings not to tell their friends that they were leaving Egypt and that they would be going to Canada. Neveen told her parents not to worry because she wished she did not even have to tell herself that. She later told her friends that she was going to London. They thought she was talking about London, England and said that it was cool. She never corrected them and prayed that the London she was going to would be the way her friends described. People were starting to get jealous as the UN aid news for South Sudanese people was spreading. Not every refugee that applied for immigration was accepted. There were many rejections. Some families could not get accepted to one country but Neveen's family were accepted to two countries.

There were negative emotional sentiments within the South Sudanese community itself in Egypt because of the UN rejection of some families' immigration applications. Families that were accepted by the UN kept the news of their emigration quiet. They only shared it on the day they were leaving or a couple of days before. They wanted to avoid anything that would sabotage their travel plans and they were fearful of what Egyptians or jealous South Sudanese people would do. Leaving Egypt was like the scene from the Bible where God helped the children of Israel leave Egypt and cross the Red Sea. The Western World was the Promised Land.

Neveen and her siblings were taught Canadian eating etiquette as people didn't use their hands to eat like Sudanese and Egyptians. Since her father was familiar with things in the Western World, he was guiding the family and teaching them the Western culture. He taught them greetings and children's songs in English. Everything was backwards for Neveen. Arabic was written from right to left while English was left to right. She was accustomed to using her hands to eat after washing them but she was taught to eat with cutlery. The weather was hot in Egypt and people wore light jackets on cold nights only during some seasons. Her father was talking about jackets, sweaters, gloves, scarves and hats for daily wear in Canada. He was even talking about artificial heat. Neveen was so scared and felt like she was going to another planet. The only comfort she had was that she was traveling with her parents and siblings unlike some refugees who had to be split from their families and travel alone.

The family told the community the day before leaving although some of the family friends knew earlier. They did not want people to think something bad had happened to them and they wanted to say goodbye. It was an extremely difficult and very emotional experience for everyone. People encouraged the family and wished them well.

Chapter 7.

Coming to North America

Neveen and her family were all set and ready to come to North America. They had their landed immigrant documents and had permanent residency to Canada. This was the first time that Neveen had been on an airplane in her life. They flew with KLM Airlines which was known as the best in Egypt and the world! It has remained to be Neveen's favourite airline company. It was an extremely luxurious experience for Neveen and her family. The flight attendants looked stylish

Beauty from the Ashes of War

and cool. The food was amazing and the movies were so entertaining. The family went to the Netherlands and landed in Amsterdam. They took a flight to Toronto and were greeted by a UN aid worker who gave them winter jackets and welcomed them to Canada. Everything was going so fast. They took a small plane from Toronto to London.

It was a snowy day in London and Neveen remembered her friends saying that Canada was like a refrigerator. She asked the aid worker if they could go outside. The worker said they were outside. Neveen was fearful and started to panic. She wanted heat and the sun. It was very cold. They were driven to the Global House in London and were welcomed by a very kind black woman from Jamaica who prepared a hot meal for them. The kitchen had so much food and people ate at any time. The television was in color, unlike the one in Egypt which was black and white. People talked like they were whispering to each other, in a calm and slow way. Things were slow and boring.

Neveen wrote letters to all her friends to tell them that she had arrived safely in London and let them know how much she already missed them. The next day many different aid workers came over and they did a lot of paperwork. There was also a South Sudanese elder wearing a cowboy hat that came to welcome the family to London. Neveen was excited to meet the elder and wanted to know if he had any children so she could make new friends. Unfortunately, the elder's children were in Egypt. Neveen was excited to hear that there was a South Sudanese family that lived in London and they had children but they only had a boy that was closer to her younger brother's age. They had immigrated to Canada from Italy and only spoke Italian and English and not Arabic. Neveen lost all hope of finding a South Sudanese girl that could be her friend.

On the second day, Neveen's parents told them that they had found a house and that they would be going to school right away. Aid workers took the family around to the grocery store, doctor's office, church and the nearest Catholic School to the house. They moved to their new house on Third Street and Neveen went to John Paul II Secondary School which was within walking distance from her home.

Neveen loved the neighborhood because there was a basketball court behind the house. She had her own room for the first time in her life and she was able to organize her personal belongings the way she wanted. John Paul II Secondary School also had a basketball team and Neveen was told she could try out at the beginning of the new school year. She soon discovered that her friends back in Egypt did not know much about anything as Neveen and her family lived in a house and not an igloo. In fact, she never saw an igloo anywhere in Toronto or London. She made sure that she told them this in her next letter.

Neveen's father bought her and her siblings bicycles. She did not know how to ride a bike but she was able to learn quickly. She rode the bike to school every day. Her brother loved all the new experiences and he even tried to teach Neveen how to roller blade. Neveen had a couple of nasty falls after which she did not want to learn anymore. There were not many black people in London. Neveen was often very excited when she saw black people. At school, she met a couple of nice African girls from Uganda. She became friends with them and they taught her a lot and helped her integrate into the school regime. School was very different. Students spent the entire day at school. They also only learned four subjects per day and not seven as she had before. Girls wore makeup, fancy hairstyles and even inappropriate clothing like tank tops and clothes that showed their bellies like they were going to a night club. Neveen had a serious communication problem with people because of the language barrier and culture shock. She often spoke Arabic to people and acted out what she was trying to say. It was frustrating at times but people found her funny and appreciated the efforts she was putting into communicating with them.

Neveen went to ESL classes to learn English as a second language. She really wanted to study her favourite subject which was science. The English was too difficult so she decided that she would do whatever it took to learn the language as quickly as possible. She went to the library daily and picked up tapes

Beauty from the Ashes of War

and books to learn English. She also watched cartoon movies and learned lyrics to songs. Neveen wanted to pronounce the words properly so she did not really want to learn English from her father who had an African accent. Instead, she wanted to learn it from Caucasians so she could sound like them. Caucasians spoke English like they had a cold. Neveen was observing how the words were pronounced and practiced a lot. She practiced conversations and listened to conversational tapes. She was also getting a lot of practice at ESL. Immigrating to Canada made Neveen lose yet another year of school. She was now 2 grades behind. Luckily she had started school younger than her age group so she was only a year older than her classmates in Canada.

Neveen and her family came to Canada in April and school was over that June. She was happy to learn that the school offered summer courses because all the students knew how to type and use computers. Neveen was not used to computers at all, she had never even seen one before. Feeling so behind she did not want to be the only person who did not know how to use them so she took a computer course in summer school. It was very challenging for her. She could not comprehend the instructions and assignments and she struggled a lot in class. The teacher was finding it hard to communicate with her and keep her up to speed as she was slowing the class down. He told her that since she just came to Canada, she should enjoy the country and have the summer off. Neveen asked the teacher to write it down in a letter to her father because she could not understand what he was saying. When her father explained it to her, Neveen was very upset because she felt the teacher thought that she was stupid, even too dumb to understand what he was explaining. The next day, Neveen went off on the teacher in Arabic and told him that she would show him that she was not stupid. Neveen's family did not own a computer at home so she took a piece of cardboard and drew the keyboard on it to practice at home. She came very early to the school and practiced on the library's computer. The teacher was very impressed with her efforts in both English and computers and told her that she worked like a machine. She was nicknamed 'Neveen the machine'. She finished the course with a 78% average and was very proud of herself. The teacher knew that education was very important to Neveen and that she was a go-getter. She was particularly proud because some of the Canadian students who spoke English fluently and even had a computer in their homes had lower grades than she did.

By the end of the summer Neven could speak English fluently. All her ESL teachers were very impressed. She did not need a translator and she had an Arabic English dictionary for the more difficult vocabulary. She did not want to waste any more time and did not want to fall behind because she felt she was already 2 years behind.

Basketball tryouts were starting in a couple of weeks and Neveen was super excited about it. In Egypt everyone who had the desire to play was given an opportunity. Neveen was nervous about the tryouts because everyone else was also nervous about it. She started getting worried about the possibility of not making the team. One of the African girls whom she had met was also trying out. Neveen started reminding herself that she was the captain of her team in Egypt and she could handle competition! She was very happy to find out that she and her friend both made the team. It was a joyful day for Neveen. She was overjoyed to get her uniform and already started feeling like an NBA player. They did not have uniforms like these in Egypt, there the team only had T-shirts.

Neveen's parents were not fans of her basketball hobby. They made life difficult for her. Her father wanted her to focus on her studies and her mother wanted her to help out with chores in the house. Neveen was often tired from practice and had homework every day. Every time she came from practice she was yelled at for one reason or the other. She could not practice much outside of school because the weather was cold. In addition to that, her mother would always say that there was a time for everything and Neveen needed to make time for helping the family out. Whenever the team went to tournaments, Neveen could not go because her parents did not want her to be too far and could not afford the expenses of the hotel and buying food outside the home. They were very strict and often reminded her that the family had to pay the airline tickets money back so that they were not returned to Egypt. Her family's financial literacy was very low.

Neveen was a bench player and did not play in the game much. Her parents eventually killed her basketball dream. There was something that Neveen valued more than basketball and that was peace. She did not like all the nagging and control that her parents exhibited, especially her mother. Her father was finding it difficult to get a job because he was over-qualified for everything. Her mother was working at a pig farm because she wanted the family to have money. She did not like the job but she had a survival attitude as well as trying to demonstrate humility to her family. They were on welfare but still had to send money monthly to support Neveen's cousin and relatives in Sudan and Egypt.

People at home looked at the family as rich because they were in Canada and therefore had an obligation to help them. After all, they heard that the family was getting free money and did not have to work. They did not understand the challenges the family had to face with paying back the loan, paying for school supplies and fees, buying winter clothing, bus passes to get around and buying food, especially lunches as the school required lunch, juice and snacks every day. If the children did not take lunch to school, Neveen's parent were called and asked to bring lunch to school cautioning that if they did not, the children would be taken away and put into foster care. That idea frightened the family. In Egypt and Sudan, if the student's family could not afford lunch, they would eat when they got home. That was not the case in London. If the family could not afford to provide food, children were removed from the home and were given access to services through a Children's Aid Society. This government organization's mandate is to focus of the welfare of children and to place them in a safe environment where they can have their basic needs met. Not having food at home was not tolerated in Canada for any reason. Food Banks were also available for families who could not afford to buy food.

The first year was very stressful for the family. Neveen and her brothers had to help their parents. They worked during the weekends at a ginseng farm outside of London. They were paid $60 per day for a 10 hours shift. They worked with different people from different ethnic backgrounds. They would wake up at 4 am as usual and be ready at the pickup stop at 5 am. They would start work at 6 am and would come home at 6 pm. They had one hour of unpaid lunch and two fifteen minutes breaks. One day there was a fight at the farm where the people fighting pulled out knives and were stabbing each other. When Neveen told her parents about the incident, they never went back to work at that farm.

Neveen's father talked to the black families that were living in London and encouraged them to start an African organization. He did a lot of research and explained the benefits of having an organization in Canada and in London. One of the elders, even though he was a Canadian citizen, was having a hard time bringing his children to Canada. There were issues about alcohol abuse and domestic violence in the black and South Sudanese community. People did not have jobs and some were not motivated to go to school. The organization was formed and Neveen's father was made the president of it. He took on a lot of responsibilities which again drained the family resources. They had welcome parties for new black people who moved to London at Neveen's house because her mother usually did all the cooking. Neveen and her siblings did all the cleaning along with her mother. The City of London then gave the organization a community centre and they were all still very active in the new location.

During the summer, Neveen went with her father and siblings to work at various farms in Leamington, along with other people in the community. They all chipped in and rented a temporary summer house to rest in after work. Neveen did all the cooking as the house was full of men and none of them knew how to cook. She would work at the farm with her family and come home to do all the chores and cooking. Neveen met a friendly neighbor who was a resident of Leamington. She showed her around and visited her often. Neveen did not like working on the farms at all. She had an allergic reaction on her skin when she worked at the cucumber greenhouse and the tomato farm had rats in addition to the pay being poor. She did not mind working at the apple farm but it was a short season. She worked mostly at Mastron's and loved it. There were many teenagers that worked there packing tomatoes and peppers. Leamington is the tomato capital of Canada and most people in the area farmed tomatoes. Neveen loved the atmosphere and was even able to listen to music while packing. Time flew by and she was very well paid. This was where she worked during the following summers.

People loved Neveen's hair at school, church and in public. They would often admire it and ask her if they could touch it. They asked a lot of questions to learn about her hair, not to make fun of it. Some people even asked her if she could do their hair in braids like hers. Neveen's confidence was boosted when she discovered the hit television show Moesha starring Brandy. Neveen had never seen black people on television like that before. It was a series geared towards teenagers that featured Moesha Mitchelle who had to spend her time juggling school, friendship and romance. Neveen loved Moesha's hair and fashion style. She often did her braids to look like hers', feeling proud and empowered to have someone to identify with. She discovered black magazines and started to appreciate fashion and beauty. These all contributed to Neveen regaining her confidence which resulted in her becoming a beauty and fashion icon at school. She was featured in John Paul II Secondary School's year book for her braids. Students would come and ask her to braid their hair for money; surprisingly not only black people but people from different races.

Neveen started her "hair" business using a barter system. Some of the students had jobs at the mall in clothing stores. Neveen would trade them services for clothing she liked at the stores where they worked; clothing that her parents could not afford to buy. She wanted a win-win deal. Students had discounts from the stores enabling Neveen to build her wardrobe in exchange for braiding services which would take her anywhere from 30 minutes to 8 hours for long and small braids. Neveen enjoyed the happiness she brought to customers and they always brought her more customers. She loved changing her hair a lot and she experimented with all kinds of braids. She had different sizes, lengths, textures and colors, always wanting something different.

Neveen wanted to have her hair done professionally in a salon but Caucasian hairstylists did not know what to do with her hair. She would often go to salons and they could not even wash her hair! At one point she had a relaxer done which the Caucasian hairstylist applied with a tint brush. This procedure ended up burning Neveen's scalp. Her hair was rinsed but wasn't relaxed at all. She ended up having to pay $80 (which was almost the equivalent of her doing 2 people's braids). Neveen hated the way she looked and decided to do her own relaxer even though she did not have prior experience in doing it. She bought a relaxer kit and did her own hair but in so doing, she over processed her hair and further burnt her scalp! She also had severe hair loss with it coming out of her scalp in chunks ending up with having bald spots. It was a most frustrating and scary experience so she went back to the braids until she was introduced to an African lady who had a black hair salon. The lady was able to do her hair and it was successfully straightened that time but Neveen could not style it or afford to get her hair done regularly, so she just stuck with the braids and learned to live within her means.

One day, Neveen's mother was going to work as she had gotten a new job at the Western Hotel in downtown London as a housekeeper. As the bus reached Richmond and Dundas, a passenger got on the bus with an expired transfer. The bus driver asked the passenger to pay and get a new transfer. Unbeknownst to the driver, the passenger was a mental patient. He pulled a knife and started stabbing the bus driver. Neveen's mother was shocked as she watched people trying to get off the bus and save themselves. In Sudan, no one would die in the middle of people in the community.

Neveen's mother attacked the passenger and as he was not expecting it, he dropped the knife. She wrestled with him on the ground, then two other men came to pin the man down as emergency vehicles were approaching the scene. She took her uniform and used it to cover the stab wounds of the bus driver and applied pressure in order to stop the bleeding. The EMS rushed the bus driver to the hospital as the police proceeded to interview Neveen's mother as well as all the other witnesses at the scene.

Neveen was in Leamington with her father and siblings, relaxing in the living room at the time of the incident as it was their day off from the farm. Neveen turned on the TV exactly when a breaking news report of the incident came on. Neveen saw her mother covered in blood as well as police and many emergency vehicles. She started panicking and thought that someone was trying to pin a murder or some type of a crime on her mother. She had seen that type of situation happening to many South Sudanese people in Egypt. Even though she did not know what was going on, she knew that her mother would never injure or kill anyone. She called her brother to watch the news on TV and relayed the news to him. Everyone was unnerved at that point, not knowing what was going on. Neveen called 911 for the first time ever and told them about what she saw. The communication was difficult because they spoke fast and as Neveen was almost hysterical, telling them what she thought was going on. They asked her if she was reporting a murder. Neveen did not even know what that word meant but she said yes.

Beauty from the Ashes of War

Police cruisers arrived at their location in Leamington in record time and the situation went out of control very quickly. The police were pointing their guns and asking what was going on since they thought there was a crime in progress. As Neveen started explaining to them what happened and as she was crying, they realized that she was talking about something that had happened in London and it was on the News. They then called the London police and found out what had happened after Neveen told them her mother's name. They explained to her that her mother was a hero and no one had died. Neveen started to calm down and stating that was more like it. Everyone laughed afterward as they all went home to London to hear the story.

When her mother got to the hotel for her shift, there were so many reporters and news trucks at which point the hotel management were informed about what had transpired. The story made front page news multiple times that week. It was amazing publicity for the hotel. They gave her mother an award which was only given to two people, including her, in the history of the hotel. The phone was ringing off the hook with reporters and schools were inviting her to talk to the students about heroism and what happened on the bus. She received multiple awards from the City of London, the Police Department, and also received a lifetime bus pass from London Transit. The Carnegie Hero Fund Commission in Pittsburgh, United States also gave her a monetary award for an extraordinary act of heroism. It was a huge honour for the South Sudanese community and it was celebrated worldwide. Her mother does not really like the spot light but every time she used the bus pass to get on the bus, the driver would stop and recognize her in the bus as the hero that saved the bus driver that was stabbed. People would clap and hug her. It was too much attention for her. She started paying the bus fare to avoid the attention until the story died a little. She said that she did not do it to get recognition but because someone needed help and she was blessed to be in the position to help them.

Neveen's mother then gave birth to her youngest daughter. Neveen had always wanted a sister that she could play and perform dances with at cultural functions. However, their relationship was more like a mother-daughter relationship due to the huge gap in age.

After making various applications, Neveen was accepted to Fanshaw College in London and St. Clair College in Windsor. Because a lot was going on in the home at the time, Neveen felt she needed a break from all of it so she took her exams early and was able to leave London. After graduating high school, Neveen moved to Windsor, Ontario to attend St. Clair College to study Business Administration. Culture shock hit her when she got there. It was almost as if she had moved to Detroit, Michigan in the United States. The two cities are border cities and many Americans came to Windsor to go to the Casino and to night clubs as the legal drinking age in Ontario was 19 while in Detroit it was 21. The exchange rate was amazing as well and it gave American visitors more purchasing power. Neveen was very fascinated by the African-Americans. She loved their hair, fashion style and skin tone. Some of them were even darker than she was and they were ok with their skin tone as was everyone else. Americans were treated like first class citizens in Windsor. Everyone was happy to see them. They were friendly and spent a lot of money on everything. They would spend money lavishly and tip people as if the money grew on trees. Neveen wished that her parents had moved to New York because she wanted to look like the African-Americans. She was thankful however that since she could not go to America, God brought America to her.

Neveen started to contemplate her life and her situation in Windsor. She was planning to major in accounting at St. Clair but started to think about life after graduation and who would hire her to work. She was worried about student loans as she would have to pay them beginning 6 months after graduation and finding jobs was already difficult as it was.

Her father could not get a job even with all his degrees and a PHD. These concerns then stimulated Neveen thinking more like her mother. Americans loved Neveen's braids and they would ask her who did them and how much it cost. Neveen saw an amazing business opportunity and decided to take a year off from school to figure out her next move but in the meantime she was braiding people's hair at her house while working at a Tim Horton's in the Devonshire Mall in Windsor. She figured that the mall would be the best place to find customers and build a clientele. After all, her work spoke for itself!

Neveen used herself as a model and did her hair in micro braids to the middle of her back and often used light blue highlights with black braids. Colors like blue were not common for braiding hair in Windsor or Detroit at the time. Neveen wanted to draw attention to her braiding skills and generate demand. Heads were turning everywhere when Neveen walked down the street or took the bus. Her hair was admired by many, but there were a few people who laughed at it and though that it was weird.

Neveen did not care because she was able to top it up with new clothing from the mall. The barter days were over for Neveen. People were paying up to $300 for her braiding services and she was highly encouraged by Americans because they would even tip $50 on top of that. Neveen made a lot of friends easily at the mall. People would always come and say hi and want to be served by her at the coffee shop. She welcomed the friendly approach and made everyone a friend. She encouraged them to come to the coffee shop to see her and she gave them discounts. She often brought coffee and food to the staff at her favourite stores.

Neveen was a bargain hunter and a very good negotiator. She made friends with the managers and assistant managers of her favourite stores and was able to get staff discounts. 'Happy' was a two way street for Neveen and the retail stores' staff. Neveen purchased clothing from every store at least once a week and she also referred many customers to the stores. She offered good discounts to the staff as well for her braiding services which was now a rapidly growing business. She also wanted to learn other hairstyles besides braiding as clients were asking her to relax their hair and for styles that she was not confident doing or ones she had no idea how to do.

Neveen decided to go to beauty school since she was so passionate about it and was already making money doing it. Her father was not the biggest fan of the idea but Neveen convinced him with her points about the job and she told him that it was temporary to survive and save money to go to college. Her father was supportive, even getting his hair cut by her every time he visited her in Windsor from London.

Neveen practiced hard at school on her mannequin and on people who trusted her. She learned to do different textures, colors and styles. Clubbing was Neveen's nightly activity. She found it to be an excellent opportunity to connect with people for her hairstyling services and to have fun at the same time.

Beauty from the Ashes of War

Neveen visited every club in Windsor on a nightly basis with different friends and kept her eyes on the prize which was promoting her business to both men and women. Guys also got braids and Neveen's prices were very competitive as she performed services from home thus having very low overhead. Neveen built enough of a customer base that she quit working at Tim Horton's, but maintained her relationship with the stores. Life was beyond amazing for Neveen.

While she was at school, her mother told Neveen that she was going to be recognized by the Governor General of Canada, Adrianne Clarkson, for what had happened with the bus driver. She was invited to Ottawa with her family to a reception where Canadian heroes were recognized with a Medal of Bravery. She was among the 45 Canadians honored at an investiture ceremony at Rideau Hall in Ottawa. Her mother wanted her to come. Neveen told the school about the opportunity as it was to take place during the week and she was given permission to go. Neveen took the Greyhound to London and they all traveled together to Ottawa. This was a very special moment for Neveen, not only because of the award but because it was the only time that she saw her parents kiss in public. It was uncomfortable but also beautiful. Ottawa was much colder during that time than London or Windsor. Neveen shared a room with her parents and the next day all the heroes were picked up in a bus and were taken to the reception. Neveen saw the Queen's guards live for the first time. It was amazing

Beauty from the Ashes of War

and was well-attended by dignitaries and the media. The stories that Neveen heard were so inspiring. This was the best moment and memory Neveen has of being with her parents. Her mother lifted all of the family members' heads in the community and that was what her parents had always talked about in terms of bringing honour and not shame to the family. Her mother led by example in her actions towards the bus driver.

Neveen went back to school and was inspired to bring honour to herself and her family. She won the Valentine's Day hairstyling competition and graduated a month early with Honors and the High Fashion Creation award. While in hairstyling school, she apprenticed in two hair salons.

Things were not going well at home in London. Neveen's mother opened a convenience store near the Greyhound bus station and was also selling Sudanese food. Customers would buy things on credit and not pay her back. Her father was not good with business and her brothers started to get in trouble.

The environment was stressful and chaotic. Neveen's special needs brother was also having behavioral issues at school and was being bullied. It was aggravating the rest of her siblings attending school with him as they were being bullied too. The situation was serious and her father wanted to do something about it. He asked the family to move to Ottawa where his education and experience would be recognized and he could get a good job. Her mother was not in agreement with that. There was still a lot of debt from the plane tickets from Egypt and the kids had needs that welfare and disability allowances could not pay for. The family had serious financial struggles and Neveen's mother started driving a cab for extra income to support the family. It was frustrating for Neveen because her parents could not come to an agreement and were in conflict. Neveen saw the situation and she felt sorry for her younger siblings. She wanted them to live in a structured environment and have a better quality of life than they were experiencing. She talked to her parents and told them that she wanted to help at least take care of her infant sister and twelve year old brother. It was not uncommon for siblings to do that in Africa. They went to the London Superior Court and voluntary custody was given to Neveen.

Problems continued to escalate between Neveen's parents and the environment was toxic. They fought all the time in front of the kids and everywhere else. Neveen wanted to take care of all her siblings permanently as her parents were going through a very ugly separation. Her parents decided that her father would move to Ottawa to find a job and her mother would stay in London working. Her mother believed that "a bird in the hand was better than a hundred in a tree!" They also decided that the older kids could decide where they wanted to stay and they would divide the rest. Neveen asked her parents to keep all the kids until everyone figured out their next move.

Neveen worked as hard as she could to support herself and her siblings but the money was simply not enough to take care of them. She went on welfare and applied to Windsor housing. This was government-funded housing for low income families in the west side of Windsor. The neighborhood reminded her a lot of Sudan and she had good relationships with the neighbors. One day when Neveen went to work, she had a babysitter watching her siblings. African kids are not the same as kids from other races. They are taught to be independent and responsible. She wanted the babysitter to really watch her disabled brother closely as he had a high risk of AWOLing.

The babysitter took him to the basketball court which was in the neighborhood. As Neveen had warned, he AWOLed and the sitter did not know what happened and where he went. She contacted Neveen while Neveen was in the middle of a hair braiding service. Neveen had to stop the service and attend to the emergency. Thankfully, the client was understanding. Neveen was 'freaking out', looking for her brother everywhere. She finally got a call from the Windsor Police to come and get her brother from the police station. When Neveen got there, her brother was there and so was Children's Aid. Neveen was petrified. The police said that her brother got on the bus and wanted to go to Ottawa where her father was

111   *Beauty from the Ashes of War*

living. The bus driver though he wanted to go to Ottawa Street in Windsor and was giving him directions. He did not have any money and was not making sense. The bus driver had called the police. Her brother had an obsession with the police and he would always get their attention every time he saw a police cruiser or officer. The police were in the area and he got their attention. As they were talking to him they realized that all was not well with him so they took him to the police station to investigate. From the many names he gave them, they were able to figure out his name and read his history with the police response to his AWOLs in London. The police then called Children's Aid Society to take it from there.

Neveen explained what happened and her brother was released. A Children's Aid case was opened and the case worker came to the home the following day. Neveen told her parents and quit her job at the salon. She had just moved to the new neighborhood and did not have beds for her siblings. She had planned to go to the second hand store to buy furniture. As it turned out, the caseworker that was sent to deal with Neveen's case was one of her hair clients. She handled the case discreetly and offered Neveen and her siblings a lot of assistance. The case was closed as Neveen was able to prove that she was responsible and fit to take care of herself and the four children.

Her father then wanted Neveen to only keep her youngest sister. His reasoning was that caring for all of her siblings was a lot of responsibility and he could not get additional income with fewer children. When employed, tax deductions were reduced based on the number of dependents one had, as well as the government reduced taxes payable by Child Tax Credits which in the end gave parents more disposable income. Neveen was so frustrated with her father and at the same time was trying to persuade her brothers to stay. She went through so much turmoil to try to make them comfortable and she believed that her father could not handle the care which was necessary. Despite this conflict with her father, in the end, she acknowledged that they were his kids. He told her that a child can never be wiser than his or her parents. Neveen was too upset and did not want to hear that. She thanked God for her sister and determined to provide her with the best possible life.

She went back to the salon and worked there as well as at home. She checked on her parents and siblings and worked very hard to save money. She often took her sister to the salon to be her assistant and did her hair for her regularly. Neveen saw her sister as an extension of herself. She always put the best clothing on her and did her hair in different styles. They were happy together. Her father called and said her brother was not doing well and he wanted to move back with her. Neveen was happy to hear the news and she welcomed him back. Her mother sent regular child support to Neveen as she was living alone in London and driving a cab full time.

Working in a hair salon was very different that working from home. The expectations and responsibilities were higher. Neveen rented a chair at the salon and offered all hair services. Her clientele continued to grow and she was ready to go on her own. Neveen loved working and hustling as much as she possibly could for the day. She heard remarks from one of the salon managers saying that the salon was not a 7-11. No one likes to put him/herself through hardship without a good why. He did not understand Neveen's situation and she had to find a good solution. She left the salon and started working from home again.

Business was natural to Neveen because of the business ventures her mother had her help out in. She wanted to have her own salon and work until there were no more clients for the day. The salon business is cyclical in nature and when there were a lot of clients, Neveen did not want to miss out on any sales. She went to the Unemployment Help Centre and took a free course which they were offering to help entrepreneurs write their business plans. Neveen completed that course and finished her business plan. She also capitalized on business plan assistance offered by the Windsor Essex Small Business Enterprise Centre. They reviewed her business plan and offered her financial resources. Neveen had taken a student loan to go to Marvel Beauty School but had been unable able to pay the loan back so they sent her to a collec-

Beauty from the Ashes of War

tion agency. She had bad credit and had no chance of getting even a prepaid credit card. RBC(Royal Bank of Canada) was offering a low interest loan through a government program for young entrepreneurs and they said the loan was more contingent on the business plan itself than the credit rating of the applicant.

Before opening any business, it is important to have a business plan which is not just for getting loans. A business plan helps you create structure and do your due diligence before taking financial risks of opening a new business and potentially losing a lot of money that could have been saved through research. The ideas need to be on paper and not in your head. Even if you have all the funding and resources, it is good to use the business plan as a check list during planning and before executing the business idea. It is better to fail in a business plan than when the business is open and everything goes wrong. There are many free business plan writing tools online. Neveen recommends Futurepreneur's business plan writing template and its financial resources.

You need to at least know the answer to the following questions about your business idea before thinking about any business:
1) What is your business idea in a nut shell?
2) What services or products will you be offering?
3) Who are your customers?
4) How do you plan to market your product or services?

5) What are your reasons for success in the business?

During this period of time while Neveen was getting set to open a business of her own, Neveen's mother did not like the way the family was scattered all over Ontario. She wanted everyone to be together so she chose to move to Windsor and live with Neveen as she had a better structure. Moving to Ottawa was not an option for her because of the separation and things just did not get better with her husband. When her mother moved in, Neveen had her freedom to focus on her business. She was excited about the opportunity and worked on it day and night. She secured a location and initiated some barter services contracts with all her clients who had husbands and family members who could do things for Neveen at her new location in exchange for their wives and family members getting their hair done at a discounted rate. Neveen had a very high level of energy and was able to work for very long hours. It was indeed a win-win situation for all. The clients were happy for the free hair styles opportunities. Husbands were happy to do a side job in exchange for their wives and family members getting their hair done.

Renovations were completed and Neveen was excited for the grand opening. She was pleased with the turn out for the grand opening event that was well-supported by her clients. Her mother was very proud of her and how she had put everything together however she was concerned about Neveen's over-excited attitude and did not want her to be too naive or to be taken advantage of. Neveen was ready to devote herself to the business and was prepared to do whatever it took for her to succeed. Her mindset was, failure was not an option. She had to win by all means necessary.

The business plan was submitted and Neveen was the recipient of the RBC Young Entrepreneur loan. This was more than winning the lottery for Neveen. It was a miracle! Neveen bought much-needed inventory and was doing hair nonstop. Her customers were so inspired and were very supportive especially since they had witnessed how Neveen cared for her siblings during their the time they had their hair services done at her house.

Neveen did not want the momentum to die from the grand opening. She started a referral program to build more clientele. Her mother also helped her in the salon. Every client was given five referral cards for a free hairstyle. When they referred new clients, they gave them the card and told them to present it to the salon for 20% off their hairstyle. Each card had the clients name and Neveen knew exactly who had referred the new clients. Each referral was worth 20% as well for the client who did the referral. They could call in their discounts at any time or work towards a free hairstyle with five referrals. Every client was out promoting the salon and the demand was increasing.

Neveen rented out chairs and had a couple of employees. She unfortunately, had to deal with a lot of break-ins due to the location and the preception that Africana Salon and Beauty Supply had a lot of cash in till as it was one of the busiest salons in Windsor. The salon was located near the tunnel to the U S and close to restaurants where drunk people acted out after hours. This prompted Neveen to move her salon.

In 2005, Neveen moved her African Salon and Beauty Supply business to a prime location on Wyandotte Street across the street from 7-11. She had 9 large open panel windows with a bus stop in front of the salon. Neveen wanted to get the attention of customers in her new location so she displayed her wigs across all the windows. It was hard to miss every time someone went by the storefront. The display drew the attention of a group from South Africa who were in town performing for their production show which was being showcased at the Capital Theatre in Windsor. The cast loved Neveen's wigs and 'shouted her out' at the show.

The display also caught the attention of a photo journalist from the Windsor Star who took its picture and featured it in the newspaper. Neveen was so happy about the coverage and was looking forward to having an increase in wig customers. The article got the attention of wig customers including cancer clients. They started coming to the salon and asking for discounts. Neveen was only able to offer 25% off maximum as she was a start-up company. The stories that the women shared was heart-breaking and Neveen wanted to do more.

She initiated a wig bank at the salon and collaborated with the Canadian Cancer Society in Windsor on various fundraisers. Although they connected Neveen with an organization that offered similar services, the organization saw what Neveen was doing as competition and a conflict of interest. Neveen was undeterred so she hosted fundraising dinners to raise money to cover the cost of the wigs. She found that people wanted to make monetary donations but also wanted taxable receipts. Neveen was not able to provide them with receipts at that time and realized that in order to do so, she had to form a charitable organization. Beauty Response to Cancer was born. Neveen believes that the organization chose her when she wasn't even thinking about cancer clients and she feels so fulfilled and happy to continue providing services to her clients even after the salon was closed. It is now part of her cosmetics company, Neveen Dominic Cosmetics Ltd.

Beauty Response to Cancer Society is a charity that offers cancer clients free image enhancement products to assist them in dealing with the cosmetic side effects of cancer treatment. These products include wigs, scarves, hats, makeup and skincare. Neveen organizes various fundraisers for the charity and is always looking to collaborate with as many people

Beauty from the Ashes of War

as possible to raise more money to further the cause. Proceeds from this book will go to Beauty Response to Cancer and projects that assist South Sudanese refugees all over the world.

Chapter 8.

The Wave

Windsor, Ontario was the first city that Neveen lived in independently from her parents. As much as she wanted freedom to do whatever she wanted, Neveen was grounded and followed her parents' rules even though they were not there. She cared about school, survival, success and honour.

With the terrorist attack on the World Trade Centre, Americans were not coming to Canada as much.

One of the clubs that the Americans had patronized whose prices were in both American and Canadian dollars had closed down. There weren't many interesting things to do in Windsor for the Americans so most of them stayed in the US. The border security became much stricter for visitors so they also avoided coming to Canada.

Neveen met her children's father in 2004. After dating for some time, Neveen found herself to be pregnant. It was the first time that she felt that she was bringing dishonor and shame to herself and her family. Due to her African culture and family background, to have a child out of wedlock was a very shameful thing. She was extremely scared and confused, and did not know what to do so she told her mother that she wanted to move out of the house. Her mother no longer needed her at home and didn't have a problem with it as she knew that she was dating someone. Her boyfriend asked Neveen to get an abortion but Neveen felt like that would be even more shameful and heartbreaking to terminate a life, which one could not give or create. Her entire world was crushed at this point, not only emotionally but she also experienced morning sickness and above all, she was alone. It was extremely difficult for Neveen to understand how the man who said he loved her, who had taken her out to fancy places and showered her with gifts could say something like that. She had seen him as someone she could eventually marry, but he was immature, due largely to his lack of will to commit and to the one he said he loved.

Neveen met her X-partner in Detroit at a lounge. He was a very handsome man who was noticed by the friends she had gone out with, in fact they were all checking him out and talking about him. Neveen was initially flattered that he chose to talk to her out of all the girls who were trying to get his attention, but she quickly talked herself out of the interest because she had come to solicit potential customers and not dates. He was light-skinned in complexion and tall. Most guys that looked like him were arrogant, selfish and were players. They also had a perception that dark-skinned girls were 'easy' because most of them were insecure about their skin tone and would 'give it up' to just about any guy. Neveen knew about the stereotypes and was not there for that. She had an event that she was promoting and was trying to focus on that and on selling tickets for it. She talked to him briefly and took his number. She also talked to other guys and women at that venue. She said goodbye to him and told him that she would call him.

After two weeks, Neveen needed to pick up supplies for the salon from Detroit. She was out with some friends and they wanted to stay in Detroit for the night. Neveen was not feeling comfortable with that idea. She called him and he picked her up. They went to his friend's house as he wanted to introduce her to him. His friend was a photographer and he seemed OK except that he drank too much and talked about his X-wife the entire time. He took their photos and said they made a cute couple. Her X helped her out with the supplies and took her home to Windsor. He asked her out on a date and Neveen agreed. He took her to Chili's which is Neveen's favourite restaurant. Before going to the restaurant, a phone call came in from his sister who needed help. He took Neveen to the sister's house and took care of her before going on the date. Neveen was highly impressed by that and thought he was different. The date went well and he was a perfect gentleman. He was so motivated to help Neveen and her business. He did a lot of research and helped her find many wholesale places in the Greater Metro Detroit area.

He was a construction worker and he would drive back and forth to Windsor and Detroit every day to see Neveen. He surprised her one day in partnership with Neveen's mother by building shelving units for the salon as well as purchasing mannequins, wigs and other supplies for the salon. Neveen could not understand how a sweet guy like that could say that he wanted her to abort his child.

She determined that "you made your bed so lay in it", and decided that she was going to go through with the pregnancy alone. She told him that the only person who was going to get aborted was him so he was free to leave. Neveen started a journal in which she began writing letters to her unborn child. She felt that all she had was her baby and that her child was a gift from God. To Neveen's surprise, her partner stayed in the relationship, still coming over every day. She asked him if he was going to stay with her and he said yes. With this affirmation, Neveen believed things were heading for good days. Neveen told him that they had to get married as that would be the only way that her father would accept their situation. He agreed but she could tell that it was too much for him. He was still trying to process the pregnancy and adding marriage was too much expectation from his kind of man. He began drinking and acting out.

Neveen changed her mind about the marriage. She did not want him to tell her one day that the only reason he married her was because she was pregnant and that she had forced him to do so. He was relieved. She knew that she had made a mistake, but God still blessed her. She said to herself, "no one can buy a child in the market like a commodity" and she was ready to face the consequences drawing strength from her unborn child. She told her mother about the pregnancy but could not find the courage to tell her father because she was too ashamed.

When she went into labor, her mother called her father and told him. She asked him to forgive Neveen and to give his blessing to her and to his grandchild who was about to be born. Her father dealt with the shocking news well. When her mother passed the phone to her, it felt like taking a sword and stabbing her heart through her ears. This was the most shameful experience ever for Neveen. All she could do was cry. Her father was sweet and supportive. He told her that he loved her and he blessed her on the phone. It was a highly emotional day for Neveen and her family.

After long hours of labor, her daughter was born. The baby's father cut her umbilical cord and carried her. He was very happy that she was born and loved her so much. He built a nursery for her in the salon and helped Neveen take care of her. His family were extremely supportive and visited Neveen at the hospital and at home. They showered the baby with gifts and attended her naming ceremony according to the South Sudanese culture. Neveen loved her X so much, and because she felt everyone deserves a chance to experience change she thought to give him the chance to get it right and really be the man she expected him to be. About this time was when she got pregnant again and soon had a second child by him. They later had issues which did not help the relationship beyond that point. He loved his son very much and treated him like a golden child. Neveen's father came to Windsor and he wanted to talk to his grandchildren's father. Her X was so nervous and was asking Neveen what her father wanted to talk to him about. Neveen was not sure but she assumed it was about marriage. He put her father in a hotel near the house and took him to Detroit to show him around and they also went shopping. Neveen never knew what was discussed and that was the last time

Beauty from the Ashes of War

she saw her father alive.

The relationship was progressively getting worse and he was acting very immature. From that time on she knew she had to deal with her reality. She decided to move on as she did not see any hope in the relationship.

Her father moved to Calgary where the family was staying. Her mother put in a lot of effort to bring the family together in Calgary. She moved from Windsor because of the recession and Neveen's brother moved from Australia and her cousins moved from London to join the family. Everyone was there except Neveen and her children. Neveen could not move because of her business and her X who lived in Detroit. Her mother sent her sister to Windsor to stay with Neveen so that she was not totally alone and also to help with babysitting.

The differences in personalities, maturity level, different cultures and life goals were the saboteurs of the relationship between Neveen and her partner. The couple ended their relationship in 2009 but he continued to visit the children regularly from Detroit.

Neveen's father was traveling a lot because of his political career while South Sudan was going through a referendum in order to collect votes from South Sudanese people at home and abroad. Earlier in 2010, there was news that her father was arrested and tortured by opposition soldiers in South Sudan. People in the community were calling Neveen and encouraging her to be strong although Neveen was terrified for her father and asked him so many time not to go to South Sudan because it was not safe. Despite her pleas, he later died in the midst of the political turmoil. Neveen was devastated. She loved her father and regretted that he did not heed her warnings and concerns. He devoted everything to South Sudan and to his people. He exhausted all his resources including his family and he died because of it. Neveen had to accept that this had been his passion and he died doing what he believed in. The government buried him in his village in Yei. None of his children were there for his burial. His wife flew in from Canada, being the only person on behalf of his immediate family who was present for his burial.

Shortly after the death of her father, Neveen received news of health concerns regarding her mother. They said it may be cancer. Neveen did not want to lose both of her parents at the same time. Her priorities changed at that moment. Family was more important than having a successful business. She closed down her salons and moved to Calgary as her mother had requested.

Even though he was no longer with them, Neveen wanted to make her father proud so she went back to school. She was an emotional mess during this time but was trying hard to press forward. There were

Beauty from the Ashes of War

some challenges in starting over in Calgary, but she was able to quickly find short-term employment as a car salesperson and soon moved to a career working with adults with disabilities. Neveen wanted to be more helpful to her disabled brother and wanted to gain knowledge and experience without going to school full time for a degree in care-giving.

Neveen attended Southern Alberta Institute of Technology- SAIT where she studied Business Administration. She majored in marketing, management and finance. SAIT was very different for Neveen. The culture of the Albertans was different. She found people to be too sensitive yet very laid back. They found her to be aggressive and intimidating. Despite this, Neveen was not really much concerned about what people thought of her. She had come to school with one goal in mind which was to succeed. She wanted a 4.0 grade average and she wanted to graduate with honours. She was prepared to do whatever it took to achieve that. She pulled many all-nighters and worked hard on every single project in school. Marketing was challenging because it required group work. Some courses like marketing research had projects that were worth 85% of the total grade for group work. This was one of most difficult aspects of school for Neveen. It was the most challenging experience for her at SAIT. Putting her entire grade into the hands of strangers and having to deal with the strengths and weakness of the team.

Beauty from the Ashes of War

In the business world, one is able to select team members carefully because no one wants to have anyone making mistakes with their money. Neveen was a charismatic and inspirational leader but when it came to her grades she was a transactional leader. She sometimes had to do a project alone in 2 weeks which would normally take a group of 5 to 8 people an entire semester to complete. She worked very well alone. Having to deal with different personalities in groups taught Neveen to be an authentic leader. She valued her relationships with people and did her best to maintain them and keep them in a positive or stable state.

While in Calgary, Neveen's X connected with her and expressed his desire to work things out, even proposing marriage to her. However, at that point Neveen felt she needed to focus on what was best for her and her children determining she did not want to have a relationship full of abusive events on a regular basis. He told her that he loved her and went as far as asking everyone they knew to talk to her, and to ask her to reconsider her position. Neveen told him she had moved on and asked him to do the same. She contemplated that for the kids to have their father in their life would be good which would have been one reason she would have reconsidered her position but she had already had to learn to deal with the worst, and that was being a single mother.

Neveen did a one year certificate program in community economic development at SAIT. She completed her first major in marketing and graduated with honours. She was also inducted into the Phi Theta Kappa Honor Society. She received multiple academic awards and was recognized locally and nationally. She wanted to do Marketing and Finance as she was passionate about them. Accounting was too boring for Neveen and she had no interest in it anymore, especially since she is a people-person and greatly enjoys interacting with people. She did however take some Financial Services courses over the summer in which she did very well.

On August, 18th, 2014, Neveen received news that her X, the children's father had been shot and was in a critical condition. He later died in the hospital from gunshot wounds to his abdomen. This was the biggest shock to Neveen as she had never imagined or expected him to die at such a young age and not in such a grievous way. Despite their relational difficulties, he was a kind man and was liked by everyone. She could not fathom why anyone would want to take his life in that manner. She was deeply devastated, particularly for her children. Neveen had grown up with both of her parents and could not imagine how her kids would live without their father. The Finance courses became especially difficult because the subjects were very family- oriented in curriculum. She could not drop out of school so she chose to change her major to Management.

Chapter 9.
Neveen Dominic Cosmetics™

In 2014, Neveen was elected as president of Enactus SAIT, a student organization that created community projects with an economic, social and environmental impact. Neveen had been a project manager in the previous year, helping immigrant women entrepreneurs with writing their business plans and starting their businesses. When she was promoted to this position she oversaw all the other projects including the one she had pioneered with her friend. Neveen entered a provincial entrepreneurship competition. Students had to have their own businesses to enter the competition.

Beauty from the Ashes of War

Neveen Dominic Cosmetics™ was founded on November 12th, 2014 in Calgary, Alberta. It started as a project in Neveen's entrepreneurship class and expanded to an active and viable business. Neveen wanted to create a brand that told her story and addressed serious issues in the cosmetics industry, especially for dark-skinned women. Finding the right shade of foundations and powders were a constant difficulty for Neveen. She continuously looked ashy and did not feel beautiful wearing makeup. She loved the transformation effect but she could not enjoy it on herself because the colors just did not look right on her. She realized she was not the only woman who felt that way; many women, especially African-American women struggled with finding suitable and flattering foundations. There were so many shades of ivory but only a maximum three shades of ebony. The darkest shade was three to four shades lighter than Neveen's skin tone. Because of this, Neveen focused on skin care but did not enjoy makeup much. Every time she had her makeup done professionally, the foundation used was either too ashy or incredibly dark as makeup artists would use black eye shadows as powders. Neveen also struggled with finding a good red lipstick that flattered her skin tone. She wanted to have more control on shade selection and manufacturing.

Before the company was established, Neveen had done extensive research in this regard since 2008. She did not want to rush and bring to market products

Beauty from the Ashes of War

that were not sustainable or products that were harmful to her clients. She is not a chemist, but she works with chemists and high-end boutique manufacturers from all over the world. The company is always researching and developing new products. Neveen is very involved in this process.

Neveen Dominic Cosmetics™ is a 'dream come true' of a South Sudanese girl who escaped the war but also had the opportunity to visit some of the finest high-end cosmetics stores in Sudan before her flight. She dreamed one day that she would have a cosmetic brand like the ones in the duty free store at the airport. Decades later, her dream came true of establishing a brand. She seeks to have her products in every airport in the world and in upscale boutiques.

The Canadian culture embraced diversity and inclusion. Neveen wanted to create a brand that reflected Canadian values and also gave everyone who loved makeup an opportunity to find their right shade in every makeup product specially foundations and lipsticks. She also wanted to empower her clients with luxury cosmetic products that helped them express their individuality and style. Neveen Dominic Cosmetics™ carries top-of-the-line luxury makeup, skincare and fragrances. Products are FDA and Health Canada approved. Makeup and skin care are manufactured in Canada and the United States and fragrances are made in Germany with high quality ingredients from Spain, Italy and France. Materials and

Beauty from the Ashes of War

ingredients are ethically sourced. They are not tested on animals. Product line is natural and designed for all skin types, tones and conditions. The state of the art makeup formula is made of only water and minerals. It is hydrating and gives skin that celebrity glow with out suffocating it with heavy artificial ingredients.

Skincare

Neveen Dominic skincare is dermatologist formulated, safe and effective to use. Clients experience quick and noticeable results. Products are formulated according to skin type and conditions. Some of the most common textures to consider when choosing skin care are: hyper/hypo pigmentation, dehydration, sensitivity, pores, elasticity, broken capillaries, blemishes and comedones. It is important to choose a skin care routine that will work for you and not against you. Everyone's skin type, texture and condition is different and it also changes as the skin matures. It is always advisable to work with a knowledgeable professional to avoid using products that can damage and age the skin. Knowing your skin characteristics helps you understand how products work on your skin. Before finding the right makeup for your skin, you need to know a bit about it. External factors also affect the skin sensitivity to UV radiation, hydration, aging, and blemishes. Melanin is derived from the amino acid tyrosine. It determines color that is present in the skin and hair and varies in degrees depending on how much a population has historically been exposed to the sun. Darker skin tones have larger melanin granules than lighter tones and are also more obvious. As a multicultural brand, Neveen Dominic Cosmetics™ offers products for all skin types and tones, especially darker tones.

Light skin

People with light skin tones are fair to very fair and sometimes even have unpigmented skin tone. They are sensitive and have some freckles. They burn easily; therefore, SPF is important for this skin type. The skin also ages more quickly, dependent on the amount of exposure to the sun.

Asian-type skin

Asian skin has yellow undertones and varies in shades. It ages well as it is usually oily and does not wrinkle easily. It is generally smooth and even in texture but has lighter patches known as hyper pigmentation.

Olive skin

Olive skin is brownish or tanned looking with a slightly beige or yellow colour. It is found in the Mediterranean, Latin American and the population of certain parts of Asia. It has yellow, green or golden undertones. It can also be sensitive.

African-American skin

This skin-type is soft, subtle, and reactive to inflammation that leaves dark marks and scaring. It is also reactive to stimuli and susceptible to keliod scaring and skin tags.

Mixed skin

It comes in various shades all at once. It is combination skin and can be extremely sensitive and reactive to stimuli.

Once you know your skin type, texture and condition, with the assistance of a professional you can get product recommendations that will help you age gracefully. It is always important to go back for analysis every season as skin changes as the weather changes. Skin care in the winter is very different than spring and summer. Products that you apply on your skin everyday affect it in the long run. Water based products hydrate the skin while oil based products moisturize the skin. Oily skin can be dehydrated. It is important to find a regular skin care routine that is appropriate for your skin and that will be used twice daily, once in the morning and once at night. Skin care at night is extremely important as the skin regenerates itself at night while you are sleeping.

Makeup

Neveen Dominic Cosmetics™ makeup is water and mineral based. It is light and hydrating for the skin. It actually feels like you have nothing on, feeling only like skin, not like a heavy mask. The foundations are long lasting and have amazing coverage. Powders have dual action and are buildable as foundations and excellent for touch ups. The pigmentation is high and a little goes a long way. Neveen wants every client to feel beautiful and find products that complement the skin and look natural. There is a lot of room for make-up artists to grow with the company as Neveen views them as important stakeholders and partners. The Neveen Dominic™ platform artists' team is growing rapidly and makeup artists are encouraged to join the fun.

Foundations

Foundations are the main reason that Neveen started the company. She was dissatisfied with looking ashy and in her opinion, ridiculous, and was tired of seeing others with the same struggles. The cosmetics industry dismissed ebony skin tones and beyond but Neveen put a stop to that with the launch of her Juba Collection. (Read about it in the following chapter.)

When choosing your foundation it is important to know your skin undertone, skin type, texture and condition, desired finish and for what occasion the

Beauty from the Ashes of War

foundation is needed. First and foremost, you must begin with a clean face. Apply a primer or moisturizer to protect your skin before applying any make-up products including foundation. Before applying foundation, correct the skin if it is needed. For example if you have redness, use a green corrector prior to applying foundation. Apply concealer to cover any blemishes including under the eyes for puffiness and dark circle coverage. Once the skin looks flawless, apply powder to set everything. Neveen wants every client to have the flawless look she deserves. Foundations don't only offer even texture and tones, Neveen Dominic™ foundations hydrate and moisturize skin. They can provide both dewy and matte finishes according to the customers' desire and skin type. They can also cover minor blemishes, increase luminosity of skin and enhance the complexion. Neveen Dominic Cosmetics™ carries three different types of foundations; HD liquid foundation™ for dewy finish, Cream foundation™ for a natural to matte finish, and Dual Powder foundation™ for a matte finish. The Dual Powder foundation™ can be used with a wet sponge for light to medium coverage and set with a powder brush. The formula is buildable (a makeup artist's term which means it can give coverage as the customer desires) and easy to apply. The rest of the foundations offer full coverage. The concealers are also one of Neveen Dominic Cosmetics™' best sellers as they not only cover blemishes but they reduce puffiness under the eyes, increase elasticity, and are excellent for highlighting the skin.

Pencils and Liners

Pencils and liners are important for framing the face and enhancing eyes, brows and lips. They can be used for both natural and dramatic applications. They can also be used to intensify eyeshadows.

When you are penciling eyebrows, consider the natural brow shape and your starting point. There are three distinct points to keep in mind. The head which is in line with the tear duct, the arch which is the highest points of the brows, and the tail which is the end of the brows and should be in a 45 degree angle, lining up with the corner of the eyes and nose. Create a dot at each point of the brow and join them to complete your look. Always set your pencil with powder for a longer-lasting wear. Apply light pressure and feathered movements in the front and outward towards the tail to create a gradual effect. Brows go through many trends every season. Regardless of the trend, Neveen Dominic Cosmetics™ eye brows pencils and powder are amazing for all trends. Brow pencils are made of 70% wax and 30% pigment. Use brow pencils to create definition and powder to add softness. Use both for intense, bold or dramatic looks.

Before applying an eyeliner or pencil, keep in mind the shape of your eyes and their color. The idea is to achieve an almond eye shape. You can use both eye pencils and liners as well as eyeshadows to achieve this. The following are corrective techniques that you can use to achieve this goals.

• If you have small eyes, give it the illusion of larger eyes by applying light and bright shadows to bring out the eyes like Neveen Dominic™ pigments or Chi Chi™. Line your water line with pencil but do not join the top and bottom near the tear duct area. Also highlight the brow bone from center to corner.

• If you have round eyes, add shape to the eyes by working everything from the center of the eyes out. Focus on thickness of the lashes more than lengthening. Apply at least 2 coats of mascara such as the Neveen Dominic™ Curling Mascara™ or Volume Mascara™. If you want to add lashes use half lash and choose thicker lashes. Apply eyeshadows from the center outwards.

• If you have deep set eyes, draw attention to your eyes and bring them forward by lightening the center of the eyes with eye shadows and dragging it upward and outward. Use tight liner to line up under your lash line in the inner corner and regular eye liner. Use Black Caviar™ from Neveen Dominic Cosmetics™

• If you have prominent or protruding eyes, draw attention away from your eyes by doing a smoky eye all the way around the eyes. Black Caviar™ from Neveen Dominic Cosmetics™ is a must have along with black eye shadow from the independent pallet.

• If you have close-set eyes, draw attention away from the center of the face by placing the focus on the outer edges of the brows, lashes and eyelids. Use eye shadows that have depth in the middle and highlight the inner corner of your eyes using Neveen Dominic™ highlighters, pigment or Chi Chi™. Eyebrow shaping should be a priority beauty service. Find the best eyebrow technician and never leave her. Make sure you go for your appointments regularly and do not slack off.

• If you have wide set eyes, draw attention towards the center of the face and away from the outer edges of the brows, lashes and eyelids. Dark eye shadows in the corners to reduce the area and create an illusion of shorter and smaller eyes. Smoky eyes are perfect. Avoid highlighting. Apply Black Caviar™ from Neveen Dominic Cosmetics™ evenly on upper and lower lash until they meet in the corner of the eyes.

• If you have droopy eyes, use Neveen Dominic™ products to lift them up by using light eye shadows and highlighters. Apply tight liner under the eye lashes. Use lengthening mascaras and false lashes from Neveen Dominic Cosmetics™.

• If you have hooded eyes, Lift them up and minimize attention to the hooded area. Use medium to dark shades of eye shadows on the hanging skin. Always do a tight liner and use lengthening mascara, false lashes or both. *(Check the back of the book for your coupon for the independent pallet.)*

Shadows and pigments

Neveen Dominic's eye shadows and blush are triple milded and are highly pigmented. A little goes a very long way. Its' mineral based pigments are pure and have a glow. Clients use it on their body and hair as well and also love it as a highlighter.

Neveen Dominic™ makeup application tips for eye makeup are:

- Press on base colors so it stays.

- For eyelid color application tap. `

- For crease, roll the tip of the bush in eye shadow. Blend back and forth in gentle windshield movements starting from the center and always look straight out.

- Curl your eyelashes before applying mascara or false lashes. Look down first when you attach the lash curler. Press gently for a soft curl and intensely for a defining curl and lift. If you have very curly lashes, insert the lash curler in very hot water, protect your skin and attach the curler to the lash hair only and straighten it. Consult your doctor before practicing this technique to insure that it is safe for you to use.

• Apply mascara on the top upper lashes outward and on the inner lashes starting at the base and upward. Apply two coats of mascara for volume and use the tip of the mascara to individually create length. Use Neveen Dominic Cosmetics™ Curling and Volume Mascara to achieve length and volume at the same time.Never share your Neveen Dominic™ mascara applicator with anyone. It is for personal use only. Do not pump your mascara as allowing air in will dry it out and allow bacteria to enter and grow. Do not use mascara if you have an eye infection or any contraindications to your makeup application. Bacteria grows in dark warm places like mascara in makeup cases or purses. Mascaras are only good for three months so get rid of your mascaras every three months even if there is some left or even if you have only used it once.

Contouring and highlighting

The concept of contouring and highlighting is highly misunderstood by many people due to YouTubers showing people contouring on their face which does not work for everyone. When you are considering contouring and highlighting, the very first thing you need to know is your face shape. Contouring draws back features and highlighting brings features forward. To understand the contouring concept, stand directly under a light in a room. Look at yourself in the mirror and you will see areas of your face that have shadows and some that have light. The shadows are the contours and the light areas are the highlights. Photographers use this concept to edit photos and bring character and definition to them. The point is that not all shapes are created equal therefore all faces are not contoured and highlighted the same. There are seven beautiful basic face shapes: oval, round, square, diamond, triangle/pear, heart/upside down triangle, and oblong/rectangle.

The ideal facial shape is oval. It is symmetrical in height and width and is balanced. When contouring and highlighting, the idea is to transform all non-oval shaped faces to oval by creating illusion of shadows and light.

Use the following techniques to contour and high-light your face once you find out your face shape.

• Oval: It is the ideal face shape and does not re-quire any contouring or highlighting.

• Round: The jaw and hairline are full and round. Contour the face line in a C shape and draw attention to the center of the face by highlighting the forehead, nose and chin.

• Square: Temple bone to jaw are angular and straight up and down. Contour the corner of the fore-head and jaws and highlight the chin and forehead.

- Diamond: The forehead and chin are narrow and the cheekbones are further away. Contour the top of the cheekbones and below chin and highlight under the eyes and middle of forehead and chin.
- Triangle/pear: The forehead is narrow and the jaw is wide. Contour the top of the forehead across the hairline and the corners of the jaw and highlight the cheek bones and middle of forehead.

- Heart/upside down triangle: The forehead is wide and the jaw is narrow. Contour the sides of the face and the frontal bone and highlight the chin and under the jaw line. Do not highlight forehead.

- Oblong/rectangle: The face is 50% longer. Contour corners of the face and highlight cheekbones.

Neveen Dominic™ has amazing contouring pallets in both cream and powder and strobing pallets for highlighting. *(Check the back of the book for your coupon.)*

CHI CHI ™

It is the number one best-selling glitter dust that has driven every client 'crazy' wherever Neveen Dominic Cosmetics™ are exhibited. It is beyond a cosmetic product. It is a unique experience which you can only experience by buying one to understand. Every girl with the name Chi Chi needs this as a souvenir in her life!

It is basically the gift that keeps on giving. It is a mineral loose shimmer that you can use to add glow anywhere on your body, hair and even nails. Use it as a highlighter to highlight your cheekbones and eyebrow bones or add it to your liquid foundation to create a dewy finish.

Lips

There are many ways to add color to the lips. You can use lip liner or pencil, apply lipstick or lip gloss or do both. It is important to keep in mind the current shape of your lips and your desired look. Pencils are great for correcting lip shapes that are unbalanced, uneven, full or thin. Lips can be shaped and filled with the lip liner. Ombre makeup effects can also be created using lip pencils. Neveen Dominic™ has a wide lip pencil selection and they are an excellent base for long lasting lip makeup application. They can also be worn alone as a matte lip product or with gloss for a light lipstick or lip gloss effect. The highly pigmented gel pencils are extremely long lasting and are best sellers.

Lipsticks

Lipsticks are most women's favorite makeup product. They instantly show that you are wearing makeup. Selecting the right lipstick can be stressful because you need to select a shade that is flattering to your skin tone and you need to keep makeup trends and seasons in mind. A general rule to wearing lipstick is to stick with light and vibrant colors for spring and summer and to go with deep and darker tones for fall and winter. Every woman needs the right red lipstick. It is a must have. A maximum of 3 lipsticks for any given season is the standard recommendation. You may choose to buy a lip liner or lip gloss to create fun looks with texture and color. Neveen Dominic Cosmetics™ is popular for carrying a variety of lipsticks that are full of antioxidants and pigment. They come in high gloss and matte. They are so highly pigmented that they can be applied alone without a liner. *(Check the back of the book for your coupon.)*

The first and most important step to flawless skin is skincare. You only have one skin so take care of it over the years. There are many cosmetics counters that are happy to help you answer your questions so take the time to see someone in your local area, especially to get tips on how to take care of your skin. Neveen Dominic Cosmetics™ is also available 24 hours online and on social media to help you with any questions or concerns that you many have. Makeup is very personal and clients are offered personalized services to suit their individual unique needs. (Find skincare and makeup coupons at the back of the book)

Chapter 10.

The Juba Collection

Juba is the capital city of South Sudan. It is also where Neveen Dominic was born. The war in South Sudan put the country in an unsafe state ever since Neveen left as a child with her family to escape the war. It is her desire to go home one day and empower people in her community and hopefully even to open a factory which can employ young South Sudanese people. As she continues to pray about this vision, Neveen wanted to give a tribute to her home country and to send a loud message of self-confidence to South Sudanese women all over

Beauty from the Ashes of War

the world. She created the Juba™ pallet collection to represent the different shades of dark skin tones in Sudan. She also wanted to combine shades in the collection that represented her adopted Canadian culture of diversity and inclusion.

The Juba Collection™ was launched in New York, New York in the United States on April 7th, 2017. The launch was attended by supermodel and activist Mari Malek, and Juba Collection™ ambassador Nyachieng Gatbel and her amazing sister Nyabuoy. Other guest included Nikki French and Brian Champagne. Neveen was honored to have Michael Key, the Emmy Award winning makeup artist, publisher of Makeup Artist Magazine© and founder of the International Makeup Artist Trade Show- IMATS attend the launch and review the Juba Foundation Pallet™. It was also reviewed by editors for 6 months and was featured in Makeup Artist Magazine© in the summer issue of 2017.

Neveen was very proud of the successful launch and was honored to represent South Sudan. She wanted to give makeup artists a unique, convenient and desperately needed product to enhance their business and offer an opportunity of expansion into the African-American makeup application market. Neveen had a lot of feedback from professional makeup artists around the world and was pleased to be recognized as the first South Sudanese luxury cosmetics company to enter the international market. The Juba

Beauty from the Ashes of War

Collection™ was showcased in African Fashion Week Toronto and New York Fashion Week in 2017. It was also featured in Sheen Magazine©.

After conducting a community needs assessment in Calgary, Neveen realized that the community is in desperate need of strong leadership. Young South Sudanese youth were killing each other, all were below the age of 23. Neveen heard of a scholarship program that was founded by one of her South Sudanese colleagues from college. She was highly impressed and wanted to help. She donated proceeds from the New York Juba™ launch to the scholarship fund and now South Sudanese youth can have financial assistance to finish their post-secondary education and become assets to the community.

The Juba Collection™ fundraiser was one of the many ways that Neveen has given back to the community. She selected 4 Juba™ ambassadors, all youth from South Sudan, who shared their stories about their struggles with bullying and finding makeup that was more suitable for their skin, to represent her brand. Neveen is very proud of her ambassadors and continues to support them beyond the campaign.

Letter to the Egyptian People

Neveen Dominic Cosmetics Ltd.
Neveen Dominic
Calgary, AB
Canada

January, 31st, 2018

RE: The Arab Republic of Egypt

To my Egyptian brothers and sisters;

Thank you for your accommodations of the South Sudanese refugees during their difficult times. I know it was not an easy task for you as was demonstrated to my family and others while we were in transition in Egypt. I am writing this letter to you to share my feelings on behalf of the South Sudanese community and to also remind you of who you are as a people and our thoughts about you.

"Egypt is the mother of all nations." You brought people together from all over the world and you shared "bread and salt" with them. According to the Egyptian culture, that bonds relationships between your countrymen and others from around the world. Egypt and Sudan are siblings according to our mutual ancient history as we are both from the land of Kush. We were supposed to take care of each other. When one was weak the other one was strong, the stronger one carried the weaker one.

I continue to pray that God softens your hearts and gives you the grace to have mercy on South Sudanese people living in Egypt. We are not looking for pity but an opportunity to rise as a nation and show you what we have to offer beyond being victims of war. We love our country of South Sudan and we hope to go home one day where peace and love can flow between us again.

I hope that you can give us a real chance at survival and success in life. We have a lot of good things to offer. Can we put our differences aside and look up to a bright and promising future?

United we can be unstoppable. Let's look at what binds us together and not the things that pull us apart. By that we can retain the image of Egypt as "the mother of all nations" and the cradle of civilization.

Respectfully yours,

Neveen Dominic CEO and President of Neveen Dominic Cosmetics Ltd.

RECIPES

South Sudanese Fool - Muzabat

Preparation
- 1 can of cooked fava beans
- ¼ cup of plain yogurt (optional)
- ½ diced onions
- A pinch of salt or ¼ tsp of vegetable stock
- ¼ tsp of shamar- found in Arabic stores
- ¼ tsp of kasbara- found in Arabic stores
- 4 tbs of any of the following oils (olive, vegetable or sesame)
- 2 diced boiled eggs
- ½ cup of feta cheese
- ½ diced tomatoes
- ½ diced green papers
- 3 diced green onions

Instruction
1. In a pot or sauce pan, fry the onions with 50% of the oil (2 tbs of oil)
2. Add the cooked fava beans, salt or vegetable stock, shamar, and kasbara
3. Mash the fave beans and mix everything together
4. Pour the beans into a plate and allow it to cool for a fiveto seven minutes
5. Sprinkle the rest of the ingredients for a beautiful presentation

Beauty from the Ashes of War

South Sudanese Tamia/falafel

Preparation

- 2.5 cup overnight soaked chick peas
- 2 tbs of all-purpose flour
- 1 small onion
- 3-4 minced garlic
- ½ cup water
- 1 tsp baking powder
- 4 tsp of freshly chopped dill
- Ground paper or chilli powder (optional)
- Frying oil

Instruction

1. Using a food processor, grind the chick peas, onions, garlic and dill until it has a course textures
2. Add flour, water, and baking powder and mix well
3. Heat oil and be ready to fry
4. Use your hand to create balls with the mix
5. Fry as you go
6. Serve immediately or later

South Sudanese Dama

Preparation

- 2 diced medium to large onions
- ¼ to ½ cup of oil
- 6-8 cups of water
- 1 to 2 cubes of chicken, beef, or vegetable stock
- 1 to 2 pounds of meat (chicken, beef, lamb or goat)
- 1 tbs of tomato paste
- 1 stick of cinnamon (optional)

Instructions

1. In a pot, fry the onions
2. Add the meet, stock and water and allow to boil for 20 minutes until the meat is a soft
3. Add the tomato paste
4. Add the cinnamon (optional)

You may stop there and serve the dish as dama or you may turn it into any stew of your choice by adding vegetables, beans, lentil, or whatever you want.

Beauty from the Ashes of War

MAKE UP
PORTFOLIO

COUPONS

BOLD. ORIGINAL. STYLISH.

NEVEEN
DOMINIC

Get
LipStick
r$39.99

Coupon Code:

NDCLIP39

Use the coupon code: NDCLIP39
At checkout Online to get 3 Lipstick
For $39.99 on your order on Lipsticks with
neveendominic.com

Skincare Regimen

RESURFACE CRÈME

Botanical Exfoliating Cream
Algae and Orange
Essential Oil

Save 20%

off any Skincare Regimen

Coupon Code:

NDCSRS20

Use the coupon code: NDCSRS20 at checkout
Online to save 20% on your
order on Any Skincare Regimen with
neveendominic.com

NEVEEN
D O M I N I C

CONTOURING &
HIGHLIGHTING
PALLETS

Get
$10
off

Coupon Code:

NDCCHP10

Use the coupon code: NDCCHP10
At checkout Online to get $10 off your order
on Contouring and highlighting pallets with
neveendominic.com

INDEPENDENT PALLET

Get $10 off

Coupon Code:

NDCIPS10

Use the coupon code:
NDCIPS10 At checkout Online to get
$10 off your order on Independent Pallet
with *neveendominic.com*

APPENDIX/REFERENCES

Historical and Technical information contained in this book have been researched and can be found in the following sources:

https://en.m.wikipedia.org/wiki/Tourism_in_South_Sudan

https://www.google.ca/amp/s/www.ancient.eu/amp/2-124/

http://www.lisapoyakama.org/en/the-ancient-egyptians-were-black/

https://reliefweb.int/report/sudan/pope-john-paul-ii-message-catholics-southern-sudan

http://seshaskin.com/education/anatomy-physiology-of-the-skin/

https://www.en.eucerin.ca/about-skin/basic-skin-knowledge/skin-types

https://dermatology.ca/public-patients/skin/skin-conditions/

https://www.webmd.com/beauty/whats-your-skin-type

https://www.webmd.com/beauty/skin-lightening-products

https://www.livestrong.com/article/65941-definition-skin-bleaching/

https://www.google.ca/search?client=safari&channel=iphone_bm&ei=dU5IWqnLK5T-jwPpm5OABg&q=moesha+show&oq=moisha+&gs_l=mobile-gws-serp.1.2.0j0i10k1l4.8166.23063.0.25583.13.11.2.0.0.0.122.967.2j7.10.0....0...1.1.64.mobile-gws-serp..1.11.1031.0..0i131k-1j0i67k1j0i131i67k1.99.bF51pXJ93ZE

https://www.google.ca/amp/www.cbc.ca/amp/1.236547

https://www.google.ca/amp/s/www.news-medical.net/amp/health/What-is-Melanin.aspx

http://www.fitzmuseum.cam.ac.uk/collections/kemet/importanceofkush

https://www.thoughtco.com/the-kingdom-of-kush-171464

https://oi.uchicago.edu/museum-exhibits/history-ancient-nubia

Beauty from the Ashes of War